MARKETING IN COLLEGE ADMISSIONS: A BROADENING OF PERSPECTIVES

Officially Withdrawn

MARKETING IN COLLEGE ADMISSIONS: A BROADENING OF PERSPECTIVES

*Papers presented at the Colloquium on Marketing,
Student Admissions, and the Public Interest*

*November 7-9, 1979
at the Wingspread Conference Center, Racine, Wisconsin*

Sponsored by

*The American Association of Collegiate Registrars and
Admissions Officers (AACRAO)*

The College Board

*The National Association of
Admissions Counselors (NACAC)*

College Entrance Examination Board
New York 1980

Copies of this book may be ordered from College Board Publication Orders, Box 2815, Princeton, New Jersey 08541. The price is $9.95.

Editorial inquiries concerning this book should be directed to Editorial Office, The College Board, 888 Seventh Avenue, New York, New York 10019.

Library of Congress Catalog Number: 80-68231
ISBN 0-87447-133-8
Printed in the United States of America

Contents

Authors

Stephen K. Bailey
Professor of Education and Social Policy
Graduate School of Education, Harvard University

John C. Hoy
Executive Director, New England Board of Higher Education
Wellesley, Massachusetts

William Ihlanfeldt
Vice President, Northwestern University

Larry H. Litten
Associate Director, Consortium of Financing Higher Education
Cambridge, Massachusetts

Christopher H. Lovelock
Associate Professor of Business Administration
Graduate School of Business Administration, Harvard University

Michael L. Rothschild
Professor of Business, Graduate School of Business
University of Wisconsin

Barbara S. Uehling
Chancellor, University of Missouri

Laurence Veysey
Professor of History, Adlai E. Stevenson College
University of California, Santa Cruz

Douglas M. Windham
Professor of Education, State University of New York, Albany

Introduction

Much has been written about the challenges our colleges and universities will face during the next two decades. Very few of these writings contain good news for educational policy makers, planners, and administrators, who must prepare to cope during a period of projected no growth or retrenchment. The administrative structures of America's diverse and vast national system of colleges and universities have evolved during more than 30 years of steady, sometimes spectacular, growth, reflecting the unprecedentedly large 18-year-old cohorts of the 1960s and 1970s, the unusually high college-attendance rate of high school graduates, and the rapid expansion of access to higher education for minority and low income students. There is virtually no collective experience or policy precedent to guide administrators in managing the envisioned retrenchment in an orderly manner.

Nowhere in institutional administration will the impacts of zero-growth demographics and double-digit inflation, two of the primary challenges to be faced, hit harder than in undergraduate admissions offices. In anticipation of the changed circumstances in which they will be operating, increasing numbers of admissions officers have turned to marketing techniques in designing their recruiting efforts. A new literature for admissions officers, focusing on marketing concepts, techniques, and research, is rapidly emerging. Proponents of marketing contend there is growing evidence that carefully conceived and executed marketing application results in an improved admissions process for both students and institutions alike. Taking an opposing view are the critics of marketing who have frequently used the popular press to focus attention on the extreme promotional tactics of some institutions. These critics foresee admissions competition becoming so zealous that the interests of students and the ethical demeanor of colleges could be sacrificed in the battle for institutional survival. The issue is thus joined.

As the largest educational membership associations concerned with the process whereby students make the transition from high school to college, the American Association of Collegiate Registrars and Admissions Officers (AACRAO), the College Board, and the National Association of Admissions Counselors (NACAC) collaborated in sponsoring a colloquium to explore the possible effects of the increased use of marketing by colleges. From the outset the colloquium planning committee agreed on the importance of moving beyond the enthusiasms of the proponents of marketing and the cavilings of the opponents to provide a balanced appraisal of both the potential benefits and the risks. It was also decided that more is at stake than just the ethical implications of an increase in the use of marketing in higher education, namely, the possible effects on the overall system and on the public's interest in the system as well. For this reason, the committee felt questions such as the following should be considered: What are the various expectations that students, faculty, alumni, and society have of our system of higher education and its individual components? Is the system currently meeting those expectations? Does higher education somehow possess sensibilities or structures to permit us to know when and where marketing may be appropriate or, conversely, where it may be a detriment to individuals or groups of students, institutions, or society? Finally, can educational integrity and standards of excellence be maintained in the face of a marketing orientation in higher education?

These issues and others equally as germane were addressed at the colloquium by the distinguished authors of the papers included in this book. It should be noted that the paper "Marketing, the Public Interest, and the Production of Social Benefits in Higher Education," by Douglas M. Windham, was written subsequent to the meeting but deals with points that he raised at the colloquium. The concluding paper in this book was also prepared after the colloquium by the director, Larry H. Litten.

The planning committee sought out presentors who would provide a range of perspectives and opinions for the participants to consider as they discussed the formulation of a statement about college marketing. To summarize these deliberations, the colloquium director drew up the statement that appears on pages 1–4. The three organizations cosponsoring the colloquium currently support a statement of principles governing good practices in student admissions and financial aid, and it is envisioned that the statement from this colloquium will be discussed in the forums of these organizations, as were the existing principles. We hope that the papers and statement in this book will be of assistance to readers as they prepare to participate in such discussions. Each association will formulate its own plans for the manner in which the issues in the statement will be addressed.

By definition, participation in a colloquium is limited in order to achieve a seminar-like setting that enhances an exchange between the participants and presenters. In a complementary fashion the excellent facilities of the Wingspread Conference Center, the colloquium site, provide space for no more than 50 people in plenary sessions. Thus, the planning committee was confronted with the challenge of convening a relatively small group of individuals who would be somewhat representative of those who will be affected by developments in undergraduate admissions between 1980 and the year 2000. The planning committee also wished to ensure that those in attendance would be able to share the outcomes of the colloquium with their colleagues in some systematic way. Thus, membership associations representing various types of colleges and universities were invited to nominate representatives to the colloquium. In addition, the planning committee invited educational researchers whose area of interest is the future of undergraduate admissions, officials from governmental agencies, foundation personnel, and the press. Finally, the colloquium also benefited from the participation of five able undergraduate students, whose perspectives and concerns contributed an important dimension to the proceedings.

A special note of thanks is due the Johnson Foundation for the support it gave the colloquium. Henry Halsted, vice president of the foundation, was an invaluable resource to the planning committee in clarifying purposes and procedures for the colloquium. In addition to providing the splendid facilities and staff of the Wingspread Conference Center, the Johnson Foundation assisted with funds to support travel and housing costs for the presentors and other participants who otherwise would have been unable to attend. Through its Wingspread Fellows program, the foundation provided for the participation of the five undergraduate students.

The planning committee worked hard and effectively on the many details that must be attended to in organizing a seminar of this kind. Director Larry Litten was a major source of ideas during the planning stages as well as at Wingspread. In addition to Larry and me, the members of the committee included Douglas Conner and Eugene Savage of AACRAO, and James Alexander and Charles Marshall of NACAC.

Darrell R. Morris
Executive Associate for Programs
The College Board

Statement of the Sense of the Colloquium

Major Themes

▪ Marketing is part of the genius of American higher education. It can be seen in efforts to respond to changes in American society by enhancing access for an increasingly broader range of students and by improving academic structures, policies, and practices. Academic marketing activities have been realized in various ways: by establishing a new college or program, by revising curricula, or by altering admissions or graduation requirements.

▪ We have always had ethical problems in the conduct of academic marketing and problems of defining and serving the public interest.

▪ Marketing consists of more than promotion, or even recruitment activities. Effective marketing includes research, planning, communication, and evaluation. Among the institutional characteristics and policies that constitute the academic marketing mix are pricing, curriculum development, extracurricular program offerings, admissions and graduation policies, and the location and timing of educational programs.

▪ The environment for higher education is changing rather suddenly, or at least our perceptions of it are. A new vocabulary and refined techniques for dealing with these changes have been developed. These developments provide impetus for reexamining our condition and our behavior.

▪ We see both potential benefits and risks from the adoption by colleges of the formal concepts, principles, and practices of marketing as they have been developed and refined outside of higher education.

Conclusions

▪ The marketing problems of colleges are not essentially admissions problems, but problems that involve both faculty and administrators. Responsible leadership at the presidential level will be required in order to set a realistic marketing agenda for a college; to involve faculty, admissions officers, and other administrators in assuming marketing responsibilities; and to provide a professional situation in which to carry out recruitment and admissions activities.

▪ The marketing challenge for higher education is to define the quality and integrity of a college's educational services and *then* to represent these services accurately, price them fairly, and deliver them effectively.

- Colleges must be responsive to more than the expressed desires of potential students in developing their programs. Educational philosophy and faculty judgment should inform college marketing decisions, along with research on higher education markets and the people in them. Institutions have responsibilities to interests beyond the desires of prospective students including (1) the student who will emerge from the higher education experience greatly changed from the one who initially selected a college, (2) the society that supports higher education and in which the students will live the remainder of their lives, and (3) the intellectual traditions for which colleges are the custodians. College marketing decisions must be accountable for all these responsibilities; the degree to which potential students' desires should influence program content varies according to the age and type of student.

- Marketing research can contribute greatly in developing an understanding of a reasonable scale for a college, improving the demand for quality education, providing better access to educational services, and facilitating more effective student participation in educational activities (as learners and as educational resources for other students).

- The marketing problems of higher education are part of the broader educational problems of our society; secondary school personnel and higher education faculty and administrators will have to work together in the resolution of these problems.

- The recruitment-admissions process must be developed as an integral part of a college's direct involvement in a student's educational development. Recruitment and promotional activities should embody the educational standards and principles of a college's curricular offerings and be subjected to a similar review. Secondary school personnel have an obligation to prepare students for effective participation in the processes of college selection.

- Competition between institutions exists. Healthy competition is to be encouraged because it can contribute to improvements in the quality of educational offerings. Cooperation between institutions must also be fostered, however, both for its own benefits and as an antidote to excessive competition.

- Diversity, or pluralism, strains our understanding of quality. Diversity must be encouraged, however, through definition of varieties of quality. Distinctions need to be made between different kinds of postsecondary educational activities, and these distinctions need to be embodied in an appropriate array of certificates and degrees.

- Higher education will be the better, as will society, if academic institutions and their members assume responsibility for monitoring their own marketing activities and maintaining high levels of ethical conduct and educational service in the public interest.
- The organizations that sponsored this colloquium should assume a major responsibility for advancing consideration of these issues and moving us in appropriate directions.

Necessary Actions Related to Problems of College Marketing

1. Understand and appreciate the existing system of higher education more fully through continuing scholarship on its functions, its institutions, and its market. Educate both academicians and the public about the nature and requirements (financial and otherwise) of higher education and its institutions.

2. Clarify our understanding of the marketing of higher education and promote discussion among marketers, market researchers (in and out of academia), academic administrators, faculty, and students.

3. Organize institutions internally for effective marketing.

4. Provide appropriate training for those who conduct our marketing. Training should focus on increased understanding of higher education, as well as on market analysis and marketing techniques.

5. Establish specific norms and guidelines for conduct of market research and marketing activities (pricing, promotion, quality control).

6. Improve our methods for monitoring marketing activities and develop sanctions against undesirable practices. Accreditation, self-regulation, cooperation among groups of institutions in peer review, examination of the issues at professional meetings, all are part of these efforts.

7. Recognize and reward by financial and other means marketing practice that protects long-term individual and social interests in the face of pressures to serve short-term interests.

Specific Marketing Problem Areas
for Further Examination and Recommendations

Recruitment and Admissions

Transfer students

Foreign students

Minority students (e.g., recruitment to inappropriate campuses)

Athletes

Nontraditional students

Remedial work for poorly prepared students

Graduate and professional students

Children of alumni

Excessive recruitment of particular types of students (e.g., high
   ability)

Use of nonprofessionals in recruiting (faculty, students, alumni)

Use of admissions consultants/brokers

Educational outcomes and guarantees (implicit or explicit)

Legitimate criteria for admissions/exclusion to particular programs
   or colleges

Accuracy and appropriateness of communications to students

Assessment of effective institutional-student match

Development of a code of ethics

Pricing

Price discounting (including no-need scholarships)

Financial aid front-loading (high initial awards)

Other

Identification of the value of higher education beyond the first job

Stop-outs (students who temporarily withdraw)

Credit by examination (credit for prior learning)

Quality control in off-campus programs, extension centers

Cooperative education programs

The conduct of market research and use of the results

Recruitment of faculty

Competency-based testing for graduation requirements

The delivery of promised or implied programs and services; redress
   for nondelivery

Larry H. Litten
Colloquium Director

Undergraduate Admissions: Past and Future

by Laurence Veysey

The perspective I bring is partly that of a historian who has written about the earlier development of the American university and who is now much concerned about the survival and qualitative health of American higher education as it enters an unfamiliar period of decline in the numbers it serves. As a historian, I can't offer you technical advice on marketing, but can only try to place the question of marketing into some broader contexts.

But besides being a historian of the university, I come to you in two other roles. First, I'm a rather ordinary faculty member, the kind who has been mainly content to pursue teaching and scholarship, and whose definition of the university has always centered on its intellectual values. In short, I'm afraid I'm the kind of scholar who has cheerfully let administrators do the dirty work on his campus, and whose natural tendency is to go on doing that, basking secure in the buffers that administrators provide between himself and the sometimes unfriendly outside world. The only trouble with that formula is that nowadays those buffers are seriously eroding. I'm especially aware of this because, finally, I come from a campus that, ever since November 1978, when a precipitous decline in student applications for fall 1979 was revealed, has been quite desperately concerned over its own future survival. In response to this concern, my campus, the University of California at Santa Cruz, is at present engaged in a deliberate effort to alter its public image in order to improve its enrollment prospects — an effort that has deeply divided its faculty and students but that represents one kind of gamble an institution can take. Later, I'll tell you a little bit of this story. But this pressing local situation, which is yet one more instance of the increasingly bleak national picture, encourages me to spend this time with you trying to think like an administrator, not just like a historian, even though I'm an amateur at doing so.

First, however, I want to don my historian's cap and speak broadly to you about the past in relation to the present and the future. From this standpoint, the key question becomes: Is past experience relevant to an understanding of what universities and colleges face in the future, concerning admissions and marketing? The answer turns out to be, in some ways, yes; in some ways, no.

Enrollment Trends

Let me give you a brief look at the longer history of undergraduate admissions in this country, first with regard to the blunt fact of enrollment trends. Back in the mid-nineteenth century college admissions were static or declining at many prominent institutions in older sections of the United States, especially as contrasted with the great rise in the American population in that period.[1] But then as true universities were founded in the years after the Civil War, and as the land-grant institutions came into being with new practical aims, the overall enrollment picture began its great growth, starting around 1890. Of course the market was still primarily the upper-middle and middle-middle classes; it included in those years only a tiny but conspicuous trickle of foreign immigrants. We should recall that the high school itself was a distinctly elitist institution at the turn of the twentieth century, only losing this character among urban whites around 1920. Colleges and universities enrolled only 4 percent of the college age-group in 1900; by 1940 this had risen to 14 percent.

The really enormous explosion of growth came only after the Second World War. It is impossible to overestimate the role of the GI Bill, passed in a fit of generosity by Congress, in making the college experience in America become for the first time a fairly normal expectation among youth. Thus by 1970, some 43 percent of the college age-group, an all-time peak perhaps, were attending institutions of higher education. But I carefully say "a *fairly* normal expectation" for some obvious reasons. Even at that peak, a 57 percent majority of youth were not attending college. College had become a routine *middle-class* expectation. Although an overwhelming majority of Americans called themselves "middle class" when they were asked what class they were in by poll takers, American habits and styles of living, when probed more deeply, displayed the stubborn persistence of firm boundaries between the working and the middle classes, especially noticeable in such areas as the kinds of ambitions inculcated into teenage youth. On this score it's perhaps necessary only to refer to the fairly accurate portrayal of the situation in such films as *American Graffiti* and most recently *Breaking Away*, where you'll note it's only the single off-beat youth from a "townie" worker background who makes the leap into the extremely accessible local campus of Indiana University.[2] About recent enrollment statistics, certain other caveats should be made. The 43 percent figure of 1970 has since declined to about 40 percent, even though the number of women attending college has increased slightly, and the number of blacks, substantially. From every indication, fear of the draft in the Vietnam period pushed the total of white male youth to an abnormal high. In addition, all the post-World War II statistics of college enrollment seem so high because they include students who attended the mushrooming junior colleges and because in any one year they include a very large share of eventual dropouts from both junior colleges and four-year institutions. The percentage of Americans of the college age-group actually completing a bachelor's degree is much lower; in 1970 it was less than 30 percent. Still, there is no doubt that the period from World War II until 1970 was the great golden age of enrollment growth.

Admissions Policies and Practices

Now, what of admissions policies and practices during this long period of growth? We suddenly know a great deal more about these than we used to, thanks to recent books by two historians, Harold Wechsler and Marcia Synnott.[3] The history of undergraduate admissions went through several distinct phases. With extreme rapidity, let me outline them for you. First, there was admissions as it existed during the whole long period of the old-time college in America, before the arrival of the modern university, extending from colonial times until roughly the 1880s, a hundred years ago. Colleges then were very small institutions by our standards, and as yet they contained no full-time administration—their presidents helped teach the senior class. The largely prescribed curriculum centered in Greek, Latin, and mathematics, with some venturing into science and philosophy in the last two years. Thus entrance standards focused on adequate preparation in the two required ancient languages and in mathematics. Examinations were held individually by each institution at set times, directly administered by the faculty. They were major hurdles, whose very existence effectively excluded all but a tiny elite of the population.

The arrival of larger universities, especially state universities, ushered in the second phase, which might be called the initial phase of the university, from about the 1880s until the First World War. The modern role of the professor as a specialist emerged, making direct participation in such matters as admissions seem far less feasible. Academic administration, on a general level in the full-time sense, came into being at the larger institutions during the

1890s, with deans, registrars, impersonal bureaucratic forms for students to fill out, and the like. Still, however, there was no distinct admissions office. The burden of handling applications grew so crushing that, in the Midwest, major universities converted to what was called the "certificate system," allowing entrants to skip taking examinations and instead be accepted on the basis of "certificates" from trusted high schools. Prestigious East Coast universities, though they were growing fast, preferred to retain the more traditional device of examinations. But around the turn of the century they began to agree on the need for a practical remedy—the standardized entrance examination, which brought into being one of the sponsors of this conference.

Recruiting in the 1890s was done by deans and presidents, aided by such of the faculty as were still willing, who visited high schools to maintain the vivid presence of the university in students' and teachers' minds, in other words by part-time salesmanship, not yet fully professionalized. But the booster tone, especially in states like Indiana, Wisconsin, and Nebraska, was already fully in existence by the end of the 1890s. By 1910 the several largest universities each enrolled over 5,000 students, so their scale was not trifling even by today's standards. Efforts at recruiting students had become widespread, not excepting august Harvard, and in certain sections of the country were keenly competitive. The brochure and the catalog were already being used as calculated weapons. The University of Pennsylvania had the clear equivalent of a public relations office by 1906. But still there was no distinct admissions office to handle recruitment or applications.

The admissions office begins to appear immediately after World War I—at Columbia, for instance, in 1919. Its arrival ushers in a third phase in the history of undergraduate admissions. And in this connection a major surprise occurs. Oddly enough, as both the historians Wechsler and Synnott have pointed out, at colleges and universities of high prestige, especially on the East Coast, the ensuing interwar period, which brought the full flowering of the admissions office, was marked by sustained efforts to exclude certain kinds of students, rather than by efforts to attract the widest range of qualified students. To be blunt, the admissions office in the endowed universities, as revealed in recent archival research, appears to have been created very largely to devise ways and means of reducing the numbers of Jewish students. Moreover, this remained a remarkably constant purpose from the teens onward, ending only after the revelation of the concentration camp horrors in the late 1940s. But a public facade masked this motive under such slogans as "diversity" and "individual character." Nor was the anti-Semitic motive missing at some state universities, where it found expression in attempts to secure the opposite of diversity, by limitations on the numbers of out-of-state students accepted.

The idea of recruiting students on the basis of geographical diversity emerged as an excuse to restrict the numbers of students from Jewish backgrounds who came from places such as New York City. Without that peculiar impetus, the otherwise innocuous logic of gaining national appeal and support would not have gained the prominence in certain institutional strategies that it did. Yet the concept of geographical diversity lingered after the anti-Semitic motive was quietly buried during the late 1940s and 1950s. It mingled now with a brand-new conception, the idea of "meritocracy," or admission based primarily on intellectual qualifications.

From our own point of view, there was much that was positively shameful in the history of college and university admissions earlier in this century. The idea of admissions based upon intellectual merit was never entirely absent, but it was severely bent by the countervailing idea, never so openly stated, of the college as an exclusive kind of social environment. It was not simply a matter of trying to lessen the numbers of Jewish students, though this must not be minimized; the same urge to create a reassuring type of social atmosphere and to win alumni support and contributions led to the favored recruitment of athletes, ever since the 1880s, and to similar favoritism toward the sons of alumni. Moreover, in some admissions circles there was an actual animus against students of the highest intellectual talent, which overlapped the anti-Semitism, resulting in the stereotype of the so-called grind, or sometimes greasy grind. Using the vocabulary of searching for "individual character," admissions officers and committees sought blandly conforming students of the kind that were assumed to be appropriate for career-networks in such fields as business and law. Direct evidence exists in admissions records during such decades as the 1920s of deliberate partiality against potential students who were too greatly inclined in an intellectual direction. Meanwhile, the abandonment of Greek after 1900 made admission far less of an intellectual hurdle for those semiunfortunates whom Harvard's President Eliot privately termed the "stupid sons of the rich."[4]

I won't linger any longer over these sorry episodes in the history of American college admissions, but to leave them out of even a brief account of the subject would be to give it an unreal air. It may be useful to recall, as one now ponders the ethical questions arising from more self-conscious marketing to attract students, that ethical questions have long been deeply interwoven into the history of admissions, as much if not more in the age of growth as in the age of declining numbers. Indeed, the prospect of being able far less often to select among potential students may amount to an ethical godsend.

To return to the more recent phases in the history of admissions, my chief point about the notion of meritocracy in admissions is that it came to prominence so late. Only in the 1950s, and especially in the early to middle 1960s, did the notion of meritocracy, or of truly equal opportunity regardless of background, become uppermost in admissions practice at colleges of high prestige. As late as 1958 at Princeton, 70 percent of alumni sons were accepted but only 35 percent of those who lacked Princeton connections.[5] I happen to believe in intellectual meritocracy as the fundamental basis for college admissions, modified only by a certain degree of reverse discrimination as payment for past ethnic injustice. But as a historian I present the idea of meritocracy to you not as the grand American tradition, except perhaps in the form of those very old examinations that innocently tested your knowledge of Greek, but rather as a startlingly new dominant conception in college admissions. It is the product of very recent decades and no doubt the product of secret shame over past practices in an altered cultural climate.

If the phase of meritocracy in admissions lasted roughly from 1950 to 1965, it was succeeded by a new phase in which an ideal of ethnic representation, once again bending notions of intellectual merit, became uppermost, as the direct product of the civil rights movement. Now it seems likely that this last phase is in turn coming toward an end, partly as a result of waning interest in civil rights, but even more because the demographic picture is pushing us, at all institutions other than a favored few, toward an emphasis on recruitment rather than selection to a degree never before encountered in the history of the subject.

All this, in very brief compass, is an outline of the long-term history of college admissions in this country, as scholars would now see it. It contains much that is utterly irrelevant to your concerns as people dealing with admissions and recruitment at present. History does not always teach us relevant lessons, or perhaps one of its main lessons can be to make us feel how glad we are we have escaped from it! The 1970s, and still more the 1980s, represent a radical break with the past in American higher education as in our economic condition as a nation generally. The long age of growth has ended. In higher education we are peculiarly vulnerable to the change, for we deal primarily with a youthful age-group whose demographic contours rapidly become factual in the wake of decisions by middle-class Americans to have fewer children. Moreover, our product, the bachelor's degree, is usually conferred upon a given individual only once, in contrast to the purchases of other consumer products, such as automobiles, which can be repeatedly made during the course of a lifetime. (Only the M.A. offers us faint hope.) Even the older returning student, on whom so much is sometimes counted when the normal age-cohort declines nationally by one quarter, will usually seek a degree but once, or at most twice. And beyond the great drop in potential clientele, which is the direct result of the birthrate, a further negative factor intrudes. The composition of the American population is being altered by new immigration, the bulk of which from Mexico is in no economic or cultural position to attend college. Thus growing ethnic changes in America may well make the pool of those who might be destined for college even smaller in years ahead than the birthrate statistics themselves indicate.

The Use of Marketing

So new are so many of the conditions powerfully affecting us now that much of our own history simply does become irrelevant, only of occasional interest to scholars. All of us in higher education are truly living in a brand-new, much bleaker era, and with no OPEC to blame, only the millions of no-doubt wise decisions by middle-class parents to limit their families. Yet certain themes in the history of admissions, which I've carefully saved until this point to bring out, do have a considerable relevance to present conditions and policies in such areas as what is called "marketing." Let's turn now to those specifics.

The first point I would make is that the idea of marketing is by no means brand-new; it has simply become increasingly conscious and systematic at present. The clear equivalent of the notion of marketing was already apparent in just about every one of the earlier phases of admissions history that I sketched. Perhaps it was least in evidence in the old-time, nineteenth-century colleges, which were accused of complacency. But in their day these colleges were tied to distinct religious networks in the Protestant denominations, and local recruiting channels even then flourished in those restricted terms.

In a sense, the very creation of the American university was a marketing decision. For it followed partly upon the perception among a keen-minded new generation of academic leaders that the old-time college was missing most of the potential market of middle-class American youth—that it was failing to adapt itself to the burgeoning urban world of the new professions and business corporations. The elective system of study, replacing the old prescribed curriculum in the classics, was designed above all to attract greater numbers of students. By the 1890s one chancellor of a Midwestern state university declared his entire aim could be "summed up in a single sentence: A thousand students in the State university in 1895; 2,000 in 1900."[6] We should not be surprised that state universities led the way in such recruiting policies. For in them, unlike the privately endowed colleges and universities, rising numbers directly led to more generous legislative appropriations. Moreover, they were upstart institutions, coming from behind. What is interesting is that the state universities of the day were not content at mere undiscriminating outreach. In such states as Wisconsin and Michigan, administrators were particularly concerned to attract well-to-do students of the kind who might otherwise go to Yale or Harvard. Through lavish entertainments and other means, they strove to create an atmosphere of cordial embrace to such highly prized students and their families, showering attention upon them and doing nothing to interfere with the controversial fraternity system that comprised a major piece of bait.[7]

Likewise, curious as it may now seem, the exclusionary policies of the private universities between the two world wars were in part calculated marketing decisions. Though the new admissions officers of that era clearly shared in the anti-Semitic prejudice of the day, revealing this by the internal vocabulary they used, a distinct anxiety pushed them in the direction of the Jewish quota—fear that if too many Eastern European Jews appeared in the student body, the sons of wealthy Protestant families would desert the institution. Again, an image was at stake. The clear perception of an existing market prevailed, one that must not be threatened. As Jewish applications soared toward 25 percent, for instance, at Columbia in the early 1920s, the notion of a "tipping balance" became evident in administrative reasoning, though the phrase had not yet been coined.

The countervailing notion of geographical diversity brought in marketing in a more direct, affirmative way, for it constituted an attempt at attracting students who might otherwise not have considered attending a particular institution. Cordial relations were established with particular schools across the country. Thus at my own high school in the suburbs of Los Angeles in 1949, a "tradition" already existed that one student per year would go to Yale, on scholarship if need be, and that is exactly how I went, marveling at the ease with which it all happened and knowing very little about Yale.

It is harder, perhaps, to link the notion of meritocracy to marketing, for marketing may imply the search for a certain specific clientele, either in social or geographical terms. But if one stops to think about it, an intellectually defined clientele is every bit as specific, only less obvious because they lie hidden in more thinly distributed fashion. They are still disproportionately located in the tolerably well-off neighborhoods, since home advantages are what allow intellect to display itself on tests, but they are less accessible within such neighborhoods to the device of blanketing mail flyers. A few colleges had made a name for themselves catering to this intellectual elite for many decades—one thinks of Reed College since 1910, among other notable examples—and the change after World War II really amounted to the belated acceptance of this market by major privately endowed institutions. Increased admissions, the more serious tone created by the veterans, fear of Russian scientific and technological power, and shame over past practices all contributed to this mood. But in market terms, it was rather a bold move, resulting in cries of outrage from alumni when their sons failed to meet the new, higher standards. Perhaps the shift to meritocracy amounted to a new sense of self-confidence within such institutions, a willingness to gamble on a more cosmopolitan definition of prestige geared to the international scholarly and scientific world. Along with this may have gone an awareness that the larger, more impersonal bureaucracies of the new postwar period were themselves now rewarding talent more than connections, and that financial support did not so greatly depend in the new era upon the sustained wealth of a few older families.

The main weapon in marketing designed to attract an intellectual meritocracy became the college catalog. In the early 1950s, when I attended Yale, the course offerings in history remained thin. Large, rather elementary lecture courses abounded. By the late 1950s all this had changed. The catalog now bristled with small seminars for freshmen and sophomores with temptingly specialized titles. Moreover, it was clear that to a highly novel degree prospective students were comparing such catalogs – and learning a good deal about the various institutions to which they were applying.

But marketing was still more evident, once again, in the post-1965 period of deliberate ethnic outreach. Here was a clientele made to order for marketing, since it was visibly clustered in certain locations and thus relatively easy to reach. (Of course, countering that was its traditional low-participation rate.) The creation of black studies programs may in part be seen as a marketing device, though a somewhat misguided one, it turned out, as black students increasingly came to prefer conventional programs. Active recruitment in high schools and particular neighborhoods reached new heights.

The earlier history of admissions, it is true, offered relatively few instances of outright concern for institutional survival. It was, after all, an age of growth. But I've already indicated that the modern university was partly created in such a concern over the older college, and around 1900 a considerable number of small private liberal arts colleges faced stark threats to their survival as the larger universities gained in attractiveness. Occasionally their representatives lobbied against the state universities, though without success. More often, to survive, they were forced along the same route that is again predicted for many such institutions in the near future – accepting all students who might apply, quietly relaxing any disciplinary or moral standards, and in this fashion struggling along on minimum budgets from year to year.[8] Survival could be purchased – at least in an overall age of growth – at a heavy qualitative cost.

At the same time, however, it is important to note that a few of the small colleges, faced with this competition from the universities, adopted a very different strategy. Instead, they newly emphasized academic excellence. They lifted themselves up by their bootstraps, sought a new, more urban clientele, and became nationally prominent as a result. The three most famous examples no doubt are Amherst, Swarthmore, and Antioch.[9] Later on I want to return to this historical example of an unusual strategy to see what it can tell us about how some institutions might now face the future.

My use of past examples in connection with the concept of college marketing may lead you to wonder if they "really" amounted to marketing in the same sense that the word is now being used as a proposed remedy for the current enrollment crisis. It may be that I've emphasized historical continuity here at the expense of a certain looseness of phrase. Marketing, according to a professor of the subject, goes beyond the mere effort actively to sell one's product. Rather, marketing implies seeking out the "needs and wants of a particular market" and then moving to alter the institution to satisfy those needs. To be sure, this writer immediately goes on to say there must still be a "balancing" of the clients' "needs and desires with the institution's ability to serve."[10] And this last qualification implies less than a total surrender to perceptions of student demand. The key element in the current conception of marketing thus seems to be a new aggressiveness about actively trying to identify potential specific markets, simply because they are markets, with the implication that one's curriculum might be changed in some tailor-made fashion to serve them, along with a new professionalism in regard to the means of targeting and reaching those potential clients.

As I look back on the history I outlined for you, there was a clear willingness at certain crucial times to alter one's own internal program in the direction of changing client interests, beginning in the late nineteenth century with the creation of agricultural training and the introduction of many more subjects of study, and continuing with the arrival of business schools early in this century, the upgrading of academic programs in the 1950s to satisfy a more demanding student audience, and the creation of black studies and women's studies programs most recently. From this point of view, American universities have long been the most flexible in the world. There is less traditionalism in them than in England or on the European continent, as we well know.

One important question, as we now begin scrambling for survival at many places, is whether there are limits as to how flexible we want to become — whether, hidden in our past history of flexibility, there isn't a notion of basic dignity, beneath which we don't want to fall. Institutions may define this very differently, but it is usually there, attaching itself both to the substance and the image of any particular college or university. The idea of marketing should not in itself assault this notion of institutional dignity, for a kind of marketing decision caused many universities to upgrade themselves academically in the 1950s and thus increase their dignity. Marketing threatens dignity only when marketing wisdom suggests reduction or abandonment of qualitative standards. Unfortunately, this now often seems to be the case. Quality, not marketing as such, may be the genuine issue of the 1980s in higher education, a ticklish, elusive, often hidden issue. What is most distinctive about the new flurry of interest over marketing appears to be a greater sophistication with regard to means—the adoption of survey techniques and carefully pinpointed hard-sell devices—rather than a shift with regard to ends.

The question of means-effectiveness should be divorced from the question of institutional aims or ends—so that if one changes one's purposes, one fully knows what one is doing and is not simply letting the means-tail wag the dog of ends. A reason for retaining a careful separation of ends and means is that today the means have become so much more expert than in the past. Earlier institutional responses—away from Jewish students in the 1920s and toward heightened academic excellence in the 1950s—were based upon crude perceptions of surrounding "climate" in a general sense. There is more of a danger of means turning into ends if one has a much higher degree of certainty about the appeal of a particular substantive change one is pondering. The awareness of an external reward, now often directly related to institutional survival (which includes the survival of one's own job), becomes far more vivid.

Despite historical precedents for the idea of marketing, at most colleges and universities we are moving into an essentially new world in the 1980s because of the internal institutional pressures generated by an absence of growth. In our present situation there is going to be an extreme temptation on the part of most institutions to retain numbers at nearly all costs. Consider these figures. Currently, even in advance of the effects of the birthrate drop, more than half of all undergraduate institutions in the United States accept at least 80 percent of their applicants, and another 10 percent accept virtually every applicant.[11] Or consider my own institution, the University of California at Santa Cruz: After opening with great fanfare in 1965, it used to turn away six applicants for every one accepted, but for several years now it has been accepting virtually anyone who applies (with the proviso that all but a small quota of students must be within the top 15 percent of their high school class). Barrel-scraping is already occurring and not only at the privately endowed institutions.

Issues of the 1980s

Let's leave history as such and look more directly at the array of issues the new world of the 1980s is going to hand us in the realm of college and university admissions. These issues are sometimes inherited from the recent past, but the new competitive pressures resulting from declining numbers will at the very least cast them in a new light.

For instance, the earlier recruitment aims of geographical representation and of ethnic representation will tend to shift from a universalized to a local, market-oriented basis of emphasis. That is, for most institutions, the aim will be to forge and maintain connections to highly specific geographical or ethnic markets that promise a high reward of numbers of students in relation to cost and effort put forth, rather than to cast a wide and indiscriminate net. The issue of whether "adequate" percentages of students are enrolled from particular ethnic backgrounds will recede as it becomes clear that almost no one who applies will be excluded. The basis for the *Bakke* case and similar cases, after all, was the question of who would be admitted in a situation where most applicants were being turned away. That is why it seemed so crucial. But it is a situation that is now historically receding. It applies mainly to certain graduate professional schools, such as those in law and medicine, which may continue to be oversubscribed, rather than to undergraduate education, where all but the most favored privately endowed colleges and universities will, once again, be turning away practically no one. This is a trend one must of course regard with reservations. In a way, it measures our decline from the social idealism of 10 or 15 years ago.

Another issue much talked about in the recent past is the declining quality of applicants and students. This is not so likely to fade away. Much depends on the reconstruction of high school curricula. I would argue, though, that in a period when colleges are anxious to attract students, this will not seem to be as major an issue as it would have appeared a decade or two ago. For to respond to it head-on, by insisting upon high admissions standards regardless, would be to move in an exclusionary direction at the very time when few campuses can afford to do so. Instead, emphasis will be placed upon remedial courses for students who have been accepted. The faculty, in a time of great job anxiety, will express increasing willingness to teach in a more elementary and remedial fashion. On my own campus, this reservoir of faculty willingness was revealed last winter, just after our survival crisis had been announced, when it was proclaimed that all humanities faculty would henceforth spend something over a tenth of their teaching time giving instruction in expository writing to freshmen. Vocal complaints over this were practically nonexistent.

Still another, very broad issue, inherited from the 1970s, is the declining popularity of higher education. Admissions efforts can affect this situation only in rather small ways. Perhaps the single most effective campaign that could be launched by universities would be to impress upon prospective students, their parents, and the public in general the continuing economic value of a bachelor's degree. For instance, at my campus, the catalog for 1979-80 contains, for the first time, an appendix entitled "Some Average Starting Salaries for College Graduates." It is an honest list, and it will not make students flock into the humanities. But it advertises that, by and large, a degree still does make a substantial difference in one's earnings as well as in the type of work one does. Individually and collectively, universities could go still farther in this direction in a spirit of sociological realism. In carefully worded brochures, catalog statements, and releases, they could soberly point out the concrete differences in work atmosphere and autonomy to be found in middle-class occupations, those that require a college degree, as compared with the occupations into which one drifts with a lower level of education. Vivid sketches of working-class life could be written or filmed, drawing in fair proportion on the gamut of non-college-trained occupations and not overdoing it with lurid accounts of wretchedness on the assembly line. The constant struggle of the less-educated worker to pay off a mountain of debts in order to secure the bare minimum of possessions thought necessary for the "good consumer life" should be given special emphasis in such a presentation. The generally bleak lives of the noncollege-educated majority of the population have been amply documented in numerous sociological studies of the past few years, which need only be brought to bear for this applied purpose. Interviews with students who have tried working for a while and then decided to return to college could be introduced to good advantage. Radio advertising, incorporating these features, could be targeted on stations with a high teenage audience; advertising in that medium is quite cheap. Spanish-language stations should definitely be included in such a campaign.

This is perhaps the only way of attacking the broad problem of declining popularity, aside from the now-traditional devices of appearances in particular high schools and the like. A hopeful prospect, apart from such efforts, is found in one reverse effect of the decline in numbers of youth in our society. When this decline really hits, there will be a suddenly heightened demand for well-qualified young beginning employees in all the corporate bureaucracies. A new competition for well-trained youth will set in because there will be 25 percent fewer of them. In this situation, we may expect starting salaries to rise markedly in the next few years, and perhaps faster than wages in the occupations not requiring college training, since those jobs can be more flexibly handled by people of any age. The economic worth of the college degree may once again seem obvious.

Yet another issue promises to remain major in the 1980s — the apparent decline of liberal education and the rise of narrower training for particular careers. This is a qualitative question that is closely tied in with marketing and admissions problems. During the past few years it has seemed clear, in terms of student demand at all but the most elite private universities, that broad general education is decreasingly attractive to students, while education in such fields as business, economics, computer science, and many other technical specialties is increasingly what they are seeking. Many concrete decisions over marketing, when extended to the level of actual changes in the curriculum, will concern the extent to which such pressure should be accommodated in the hope of securing maximum enrollments.

One's position on this issue is bound to be partisan. Those who were never friendly to the liberal arts and always saw the primary mission of higher education as practical service to the society in the most direct sense may more or less rejoice at the trend. Those who, like myself, come from a background within the liberal arts, while admitting frequent excesses and failings, will be greatly worried about a resulting loss of quality. To us, it may indeed seem that the essence of a desirable academic atmosphere is at stake in such decisions.

At a few privately endowed colleges and universities, the liberal arts will remain "safe" because study of them can still be enforced as the price of receiving a degree of high institutional prestige. But the majority of campuses will indeed experience direct pressure of this kind. My own plea would be simply to give in as little as possible in each individual case, although I am mindful of the compromises that absolutely have to be made for survival in some situations. I would urge that liberal arts requirements be retained or expanded in programs that are ostensibly vocational in nature. I would urge that the question be regarded as one of balance, rather than of an all-or-nothing attitude toward the liberal arts versus vocationalism. I would remind administrators contemplating major shifts in a vocational direction of the very real continuing reservoir of prestige for liberal education in this country, both for institutions that offer instruction in it and for individual students offering their credentials to many kinds of enterprises. The most prestigious corporations, like the most prestigious colleges, value the liberal arts the most. To adopt a frankly vocationalist image is to steer one's students onto a lesser track in terms of the kinds of jobs they will end up with. It is to opt for an image related to a lower segment within the American middle class. Thus students may be attracted, and bare survival gained, at the expense of a lessened dignity. Again, American society in these class terms is far less fluid and formless than some spokesmen would have us believe. Ideally, I should add, I would prefer not to argue for the liberal arts on such a crass basis, but I believe that to do so is better than not arguing for them at all and simply letting rampant vocationalism take its course.

Differentiation of Institutions

A final broad emerging trend I want to point to is one that can't be debated in quite the same way, but one that is, I think, in all our minds as we face the future in purely practical or strategic terms. As competitive survival pressures increase within higher education, the substantive differences between particular institutions will grow more starkly visible. In this regard, it is well to note that the simple dichotomy between private and public institutions is not a terribly meaningful concept. I keep referring to a small number of private universities and colleges with large endowments and high prestige as the most immune of any institutions to the new survival crisis. They may have to trim a bit from time to time, especially in the sciences where so much past money came from the federal government, but they are in no basic danger from external threats; for them, the future is far more like the past than for any other campuses. Below them come the "flagship" campuses of the leading state university systems, where, even with falling numbers of students on a statewide basis, a sufficient tradition of legislative support assures their survival. Next come the newer, less established state university campuses, which are more vulnerable to pruning in the event of enrollment decline and taxpayer revolt; their chances are probably on a par with those of many private institutions of middling endowment. At the bottom, most threatened with outright extinction, are poorly endowed private liberal arts colleges of small size, especially those in portions of the country with static or declining populations and economies. I make these distinctions in order to emphasize that privately endowed institutions appear at both ends of the scale, in terms of strength of position, not all in any one place relative to the state institutions, which themselves vary widely. The size of the endowment and the skill with which its income is guarded are crucial to the survival of the private institutions. Annual legislative support is a slenderer guarantee of support than a really magnificent endowment, but a better guarantee than income derived very largely from current student fees. Voices that claim to speak for the "private sector" of higher education, as a distinct entity, should be scrutinized carefully in terms of the actual endowment of the particular institutions they represent.

These differences among institutions are going to be increasingly well perceived. They are going to come out in the open more, especially as a number of institutions close their doors and others try to survive through more or less desperate tactics. This reality may bring us to the heart of many of the central issues involved in self-conscious marketing. There has always been an informal pecking order of colleges and universities in this country, as a substitute for state-controlled decisions concerning quality. Actually, there is not just a single pecking order, but at least two: a cosmopolitan one based on national and international considerations of academic prestige; and a second, local one based more largely on social criteria but with some intellectual input, and therefore more apt to inflate the position of certain universities in the minds of a local or regional audience. At stake in the coming struggle over enrollments is not a mere bare survival, except for institutions at the bottom end of the local spectrum, but more often what *kinds* of students one can continue to attract in a time when there is a more relentless competition for all students. Purely local factors and factors extraneous to academic worth are apt to figure largely in such a competition.

A consequence of this complex situation is that very little across-the-board advice can be given to institutions of higher education that want to be coached on their survival possibilities and general prospects, apart from the extremes of means-oriented selling techniques. Instead, the administrators and faculties of each campus will have to make intelligent decisions based upon their resources and their current position within these pecking orders. No two campuses will ever be in exactly an identical position. Individual campuses must therefore be prepared to approach external organizations that offer them help in marketing on the basis of realistic self-knowledge. There is no substitute for their own self-estimate. It must be the basis on which appropriate marketing means are selected.

At the bottom of the local pecking order, it will appear to an outsider that large numbers of institutions simply don't deserve to survive, and if enrollment problems force them actually to close their doors, one may well say, "Good riddance! So much the better!" Of course the staffs and the faculty members of these institutions will not generally see it this way. They will tend to exaggerate their position in the local spectrum, based upon illusion and shreds of evidence. They will be the most apt to resort to extreme marketing devices, for at bottom they know their jobs, the incomes for their families, are crucially at stake. Marketing schemes that approach fraud, or that involve genuine substantive changes but of a degrading type, will be most common at this low end of the spectrum of institutions. A proper response, it seems to me, is to expose such situations with as much publicity as possible. But difficulty will arise when a somewhat flagrant tactic is employed at an only somewhat marginal institution, one, let us say, prominent enough so that from a 500-mile distance we are apt already to know it exists. Frauds, deceptions, and bending of the truth will probably be denounced, but not so often by academic insiders—rather by disgruntled students and the media eager for a story. More power to them.

A Strategy of Quality

Let's assume that all of us are instead concerned for the survival, or the maintenance of quality, at campuses considerably higher on this spectrum, where considerations of dignity and genuine concern for substance will continue to be weighed against the use of particular promotional tactics in the effort to retain students. Here, especially, the only advice that makes sense will take into account the exact nature and position of the individual institution. It cannot be general advice, beyond the level of the few bits I've urged on you, such as not abandoning the liberal arts in a rush toward vocationalism or being sure to spread the worth of a college degree.

I want to suggest, however, that there is one strategy that can actively be pursued in the context of a realistic appraisal of one's own institutional position in the spectrum and that directly addresses the problem of quality in a positive way. I'm thinking now of a number of middle-range institutions, those neither on the top nor the bottom in terms of prestige, and with some resources to give them a degree of flexibility rather than a purely immediate sense of desperation. Such institutions may well have the opportunity to exercise more freedom in self-definition than they have had in the past, simply because they will find themselves in a less static situation. When the game suddenly becomes one in which there are real casualties, risks may seem more attractive, even from a position of considerable established strength. When the national and local search for students becomes blatant, and most institutions succumb to the temptation to lure more students by tacitly lowering standards, while other, high-prestige institutions remain almost unaffected at the top, the adventurous course of action is to try to swim against the downward current. This, as I earlier said, is exactly what Swarthmore, Amherst, and Antioch, among other colleges, did in the early years of this century. It can still be done now and in fact is being done. The bold strategy for meeting the coming enrollment crisis is to emphasize academic excellence. It amounts to moving out of a locally defined pecking order, in most cases, and playing for the 10 percent of students who are willing to go to a nationally defined campus of high prestige even though it is located a long way from home. Or in some cases where the local market is promising enough, a commuter university can try to do this too. Again, it is actually happening.

Such a course of action has never been easy. For one thing, it is bound to discomfit an established, aging faculty, who tend to like things the way they are and who cannot easily be dislodged. It is thus likely to compound worries over external appeal with a brand-new internal struggle, and the internal conflict may be broadcast far and wide and damage the external image. But for the vigorous administrator who really believes in academic quality (rather than mere lip service to it), such a course might be far preferable to doing nothing or to doing the far easier thing of trying to tinker with image alone. Such a person, with what faculty allies he or she can gather, is the rare individual who will play for really high stakes — a notable advancement of the campus's position, and ultimately of its security, at the very time when other institutions are going into a downward slide while doing the best they can to disguise it.

Will true quality of substance be recognized in the long run? I think the histories of such institutions as Reed, Amherst, and Swarthmore show this. I think, in a much shorter timespan, the strong position of the San Diego campus of the University of California shows this. The only exception may be high-quality institutions that gain a controversial public image through identification with artistic avant-gardism or political radicalism. Such colleges as Bennington, Goddard, and Hampshire still do survive, though without a satisfying degree of security.

It happens, as I've mentioned, that my own institution is currently in the midst of a survival crisis, occasioned by a sharp drop in the number of applicants at a time when we were already admitting any minimally qualified person who applied. There was fear that with falling enrollments at a time of tax-conscious budget cutting in the wake of Proposition 13, it would make sense for the state to close two of the nine University of California campuses, Santa Cruz in the north and Riverside in the south. We discovered we had few friends. A front-page feature story in the *San Francisco Chronicle* referred to us as "a dream that faded." The chancellor of the Berkeley campus issued a public statement that in effect said, if Santa Cruz must be closed to save quality at Berkeley, then what must be must be. President Saxon issued a statement emphatically declaring that the Santa Cruz campus would not be closed. This made us shiver all the more because it seemed to bring the possibility of closure still more out in the open.

Why were we doing so poorly in enrollments? When we opened in 1965, we had been for a time the most popular of the nine campuses, turning away a larger proportion of students than any other. We were experimental in some degree, having adopted the decentralized "college cluster" plan, whereby the power of academic departments was balanced and modified by the power of colleges (each faculty member belonged both to a department and to a college). We emphasized liberal arts education, and our most radical feature was the absence of letter grades; instead, students received paragraph-style written evaluations of their performance in each course. Thus we appealed to a definite market — a large one in the 1960s — of students who sought to avoid the competitive atmosphere in most universities.

More than this, our image became very distinct. The founders of Santa Cruz were Anglophiles; their vision was of a publicly supported equivalent of Oxford or Cambridge. But, fortuitously, this image was sharply altered as soon as we opened, by the coincidental fact that the countercultural youth revolt of the 1960s occurred at that very time, and both the campus and the surrounding town became a kind of mecca for the participants. Unlike Berkeley, we were never deeply politicized. Our version of the counterculture was more inward-turning, gentle and meditational, oriented toward individual self-expression, often anarchistic. We had one of the most beautiful campuses in the world, sprawling by itself in groves of redwood trees, looking out over the Pacific Ocean. Nature-worship prevailed. In our isolation, campus dress customs became the least inhibited, probably, of any American college. Our bare feet became nationally famous (one magazine reporter took a statistical count of them), but there were boys who came to class or to a public lecture entirely naked except for ragged cut-offs, their long hair swirling halfway down their bare backs. To be a total child of nature and strip to no clothes at all was casually accepted as a public style in one of the colleges, where belief against any repression of individual inclinations ran strongest, and also in a famous large lecture course called "The Birth of a Poet," which always met outdoors.

These indulgences underlie the image of Santa Cruz projected by the photographs in a recent catalog I'm about to show you, for the initial response of the admissions office, when student applications began to fall off, was to play the theme of sunshine and freedom to the hilt. The policy was informally known as "selling the redwoods." Many faculty bitterly complained that the admissions office refused to advertise our academic strength, which, despite everything, was considerable, though of course we were no Berkeley.

As late as the fall of 1978, just before the survival crisis hit, our catalog still abundantly stressed the values of a relaxed lifestyle. The descriptions of the individual colleges and their programs (the less traditional or demanding academic units) took 57 pages, while campuswide programs, mainly departmental, took 141 pages. Still more significant were the 57 photographs, mostly taken by a brilliant undergraduate photographer, Mark Zemelman, and nearly all placed in the opening, college-oriented section of the catalog.

These photographs were strikingly designed to lure students to Santa Cruz on the basis of the natural beauty of the campus and the extreme informality of the life there. Though a number of scenes showed classroom activity, and some captions stressed scholarly honors and acceptances of students at distinguished graduate schools, the emphasis was on informal social relations and the uninhibited joys of the out-of-doors. If I may try to paraphrase the message being conveyed, it was, "Here are the beautiful people, simply enjoying themselves, while managing to learn something at the same time." No less than 21 of the 57 photographs show students out in the sunshine. One of the captions, with a seminude sunbather lying outstretched and apparently unawake in the foreground, says: "The Field House terrace is one of the few spots on campus from which you can see several buildings at one time — if you want to open your eyes." Some pages later another prone sunbather is shown, with the words: "A feature of Santa Cruz is that it gives you the space to pause from time to time, to pursue a subject that's not necessarily part of your major — or just to fall asleep in the sun." And yet another few pages later: "Sitting in the sun — an ideal way to use College Five's spacious quad." Even the interior shots publicize informality, such as one view of a large lecture in which the students are mostly sitting on the floor of the deskless room, a couple of them stripped to their shorts, and one student lying flat on his back.

These values did still appeal to the students who were there, so the admissions office is not to be blamed for being confused. The trouble was that in an age of advancing career anxiety and declining liberalism, they appealed to fewer and fewer prospective students.

It so happened that our campus gained a new chancellor and a new, aggressive dean of the humanities just before the survival crisis hit us. What they proposed was a radical change of image in the direction of academic excellence, partly through a revamping of the admissions office and the catalog, but also in terms of substance. They announced plans for an internal reorganization that would divest the colleges of their academic powers and move toward a more orthodox departmentalism. And they attempted to establish letter grades as an individual option for students at Santa Cruz, to supplement the paragraph-evaluations of student performance.

These moves drew extremely heavy faculty and student opposition. As in so many places, much of the senior faculty enjoyed its existing club-like atmosphere and in effect did not want anything to change. Students held major protest rallies, egged on by certain faculty, and signed a petition in which they threatened to depart from Santa Cruz if a letter-grade option were introduced. They argued that once the choice existed, students would choose letter grades out of fear and parental pressure, and within a few years we would have letter grades entirely. Bowing to extreme student emotion, the faculty, reversing its earlier approval, voted down the letter-grade option, even in the face of a brand-new survey that showed the absence of grades was indeed a major factor in deterring student applications. Thus to shift to a new image was an extremely risky course, threatening to alienate existing students and their prospective counterparts while there was no firm evidence that it would attract new students, especially in view of the continued rejection of normal grading.

In any event, the new catalog for 1979-80 launched the new image in abruptly striking ways. The administrative reorganization had succeeded in eliminating college-based academic programs, so the college section of the catalog was cut from 57 to 18 pages. The alphabetical listing of campuswide academic programs, mainly departmental, was expanded to 162 pages. But what was most notable about the new catalog, in comparison with last year's, was the relative absence of photographs altogether. Only 4 appear, as compared with 57 the year before, aside from the cover photo. Gone entirely are the sunbathers. The one large classroom scene shows students sitting at conventional desks, all fully attired, and earnestly writing an examination. The most salient message in the new catalog is the sheer dominance of unrelieved text. It is designed to attract the student who cares about substance. And it is the new image. Of course it is far too soon to know whether it will succeed. But it represents one model of change at a middle-range institution.

One fact about the recent image change at Santa Cruz particularly strikes me, in the context of this conference. Neither before nor after the change has there been a marketing orientation in the narrow, hard-sell sense. Everything has proceeded in relative ignorance of the exact student market for the old image or the new. Perhaps Santa Cruz is an example of an institution that too greatly holds aloof from the fashionable marketing trend in admissions offices. Anxiety over survival may be intense, and yet not connected with the kinds of sophistication over ways and means that the marketing tendency represents. It may be that Santa Cruz is somewhat inhibited in this respect by its being a state-supported institution.

Conclusion

Let me return to the general plane to conclude these remarks. Though the elements of substance and of image were both rather abnormal at Santa Cruz, the case of this campus illustrates a common truth — that while effective image rebuilding may seem highly necessary, an institution is limited in its capacity for maneuver in admissions by stubborn realities. Thus faculty decisions over curricular requirements, administrative decisions over what degree programs to kill or to add, and student word of mouth over the intangibles of atmosphere will all limit the scope, and to some degree the effectiveness, of deliberate public relations and marketing efforts. One might ponder the parallel in advertising. Businesses have advertised for decades, yet businesses have failed in large numbers. One of the standard diversions for those with a bent toward popular culture is to thumb through old magazines, themselves often defunct, to look at the splashy advertisements for products that no longer exist.

The key question, as I indicated earlier, concerns what actual compromises one is willing to make, either for survival or for maintenance of a student body at a given size. It is a question that has to be answered individually at each institution, given a realistic assessment of its place in the local and national spectrum. There is, on the one hand, a natural temptation to do too little, to allow oneself to go on enjoying existing routines and arrangements, even while one may feel anxious about enrollment trends. There is, on the other hand, an occasional temptation to do too much. Particular institutions will have to ask themselves: would we be willing to embark on truly drastic measures to shore up enrollments? Let me name a few. One such would be a frank, overwhelming shift away from the liberal arts to a series of narrowly vocational programs. Another would be for rural colleges in the Northwest and Midwest to pull up stakes as entire entities and relocate themselves in the Sun Belt or in growing suburban areas picked for their relative lack of existing colleges. Still another would be to move to a city, convert into a Spanish-speaking institution or at least one with a bilingual faculty and a substantial portion of instruction in Spanish, and offer most courses at night and on weekends. Such tactics all involve a severe loss in traditional dignity. They will seem unthinkable for most institutions, certainly for those that do not perceive themselves as severely threatened. It is ironic, of course, that America's leading universities have historically countenanced a similar loss of dignity in their athletic mania and their toleration of fraternities. Popularity and support can be courted in many ways.

What is likely to happen in the future is that most colleges and universities will slide a notch or two downward from their present position in terms of academic quality, while a minority of institutions capitalize on this to trumpet their excellence. At the bottom end, quite a number of very hard-pressed institutions may be expected to disappear. The question of intellectual meritocracy, as bequeathed to us by the 1950s and 1960s, will remain important only at the favored minority of institutions, mainly those with adequate private endowments and high prestige, who can still afford to turn away large numbers of applicants. Many more institutions will continue to pay lip service to meritocracy, in order not too openly to project an image of desperation, but it will not centrally affect their actual admissions policies. Needless to say, I regard this prospect very sadly.

In the scramble for survival, effective marketing is no doubt one distinct variable. Of course, if every institution jumped on the bandwagon and marketed itself with equal effectiveness, the result would cancel itself out. But there is too much inertia in too many institutions for this to happen. Therefore marketing, in conjunction with substantive rethinking, offers some room for maneuver in an environment that has powerful built-in demographic, economic, and political constraints. My fear, as a historian of education with a concern for academic quality as well as for survival, is that the pressure for retaining numbers threatens the drive toward quality on the undergraduate level that is a surprisingly recent and relatively fragile phenomenon. Therefore I'm most interested in efforts, such as those at my own institution, that seek to combine a heightened pursuit of substantive quality with more effective marketing techniques. Marketing when taken alone, like propaganda, can serve any kind of a master. One must raise one's sights, at least occasionally, to ponder what kind of a master one is serving. But perhaps you'd expect a faculty member to say that.

References

1. Laurence Veysey, *The Emergence of the American University*. Chicago: University of Chicago Press, 1965, pp. 4-5.

2. Among many other relevant sources that confirm this picture, see Lillian B. Rubin, *Worlds of Pain: Life in the Working-Class Family*. New York: Basic Books, 1976. John E. Bodnar, *Immigration and Industrialization*. Pittsburgh: University of Pittsburgh Press, 1977. Joseph T. Howell, *Hard Living on Clay Street: Portraits of Blue Collar Families*. Garden City, N.Y.: Anchor Press, 1973. Herbert J. Gans, *The Levittowners*. New York: Pantheon Books, 1967, chapters on the school system.

3. Harold S. Wechsler, *The Qualified Student: A History of Selective College Admission in America*. New York: John Wiley and Sons, 1977. Marcia Graham Synnott, *The Half-Opened Door: Discrimination and Admissions at Harvard, Yale, and Princeton, 1900-1970*. Westport, Conn.: Greenwood Press, 1979. I have described and reviewed these books at length in A.A.U.P., *Bulletin*, Vol. LXIII, November 1977, pp. 327-328, and in an essay review, "The History of University Admissions," *Reviews in American History*, forthcoming.

4. Veysey, *Emergence*, p. 92.

5. Synnott, *Half-Opened Door*, p. 221.

6. Veysey, *Emergence*, p. 356.

7. Ibid., pp. 101, 103, 292-293.

8. Ibid., p. 237.

9. See Burton R. Clark, *The Distinctive College*. Chicago: Aldine Publishing Co., 1970.

10. Gerald Sussman, associate professor of marketing at Northeastern University, quoted in Edward B. Fiske, "The Marketing of the Colleges," *Atlantic Monthly*, October 1979, p. 96.

11. Allan P. Sindler, *Bakke, De Funis and Minority Admissions*. New York: Longman, 1978, p. 29.

Uses, Abuses, and Misuses of Marketing in Higher Education

by Christopher H. Lovelock and Michael L. Rothschild

Educators have much to learn from observing and eclectically borrowing techniques and applications from marketing. But the blind transfer of this technology without careful consideration of important differences in goals and objectives will result in significant loss of effectiveness. Paul S. Hugstad, 1975

As a nail sticketh fast between the joinings of a stone, so doth sin stick close to buying and selling. Ecclesiasticus 27:2

Introduction

At the beginning of the 1970s, marketing was a term that most educators associated with the private sector, and then generally in a pejorative context. The very idea of bringing marketing approaches fresh from Madison Avenue to the sacred groves of academe aroused negative responses among most academic administrators, ranging from "inappropriate" through "unseemly" to "unethical."

But times changed. As memories of the rosy sellers' market of the fifties and sixties receded, to be replaced by the gloomy reality of a buyers' market in undergraduate education, worried administrators — or at least some of them — began to adopt a more customer-oriented perspective, especially in relation to admissions.

The more astute administrators recognized that marketing meant more than just advertising and selling, and involved strategic decisions in other areas, too. They started thinking about the nature of the educational experience, or "product," that they offered, how this compared with the products of competing institutions, and how closely it matched the needs and expectations of their "customers," the students. They started doing market research to discover what applicants wanted in a college education, what they thought of specific institutions, and why they accepted or declined an offer of admission. They recognized that pricing was an important component of the "marketing mix" and sought to de-

The authors wish to thank Penny Pittman Merliss and Jean K. Trescott for helping with the research for this paper, and Larry H. Litten and Charles B. Weinberg for their many helpful comments on earlier drafts.

velop scholarship and financial aid packages tailored to the differing situations of desirable applicants (and their parents) and also competitive with the offers made by other institutions. Finally, they came to think in formal terms of "segmenting" the applicant market—focusing on those types of students that their institutions were best able to serve, and restricting their recruitment efforts to those geographic areas that appeared to offer the best market for applicants.

During the early seventies, some colleges began to call in consulting firms to help develop new strategies for their institutions. Some of these efforts, especially those that involved a careful institutional self-study, were strikingly successful. For instance, Hood College (a small women's college in Frederick, Maryland) received widespread publicity as a result of its success in reversing a long history of declining enrollments without jumping on the bandwagon of coeducation.[1]

As news of such successes began to spread in the middle seventies, many administrators—especially some of the more desperate ones—began to see marketing as a magic wand that, if waved by the right professional wizard or fairy godmother and accompanied by suitable incantations, would transform their Cinderella institutions into princesses. But lacking a good product that met the needs of the marketplace, many were inevitably disappointed.

As the decade ends, marketing finds itself under renewed scrutiny in the world of education. The emphasis now is less on the appropriateness of using marketing techniques in any one institution than on their effect on the broader educational system. Evidence now suggests that a well-conceived and well-executed marketing program can yield some immediate short-term benefits for an institution, whether its object be recruitment of new students, raising more money, or stimulating increased ticket sales for on-campus activities. But from a policy-making perspective, we also need to be concerned about the long-term impact of marketing on the entire field of higher education.

Scope of the Paper

Marketing is often mistakenly equated with the advertising and sales functions of an organization. But as this paper shows, its scope is much broader. The organization's efforts to facilitate transactions with its customers require that strategic decisions be made in four broad areas, collectively referred to as the *marketing mix*.

These are (1) the *product* (a good or service) offered by the organization; (2) the *price* charged in exchange – how much this is and how it is to be paid; (3) *distribution* – where, when, and how the product is delivered to the customer; and (4) *communications* – how existing or prospective customers are informed about the product, its availability, its cost, and the benefits that it offers.

To provide a framework for an informed critique of marketing in higher education, we'll begin by looking at some important ways of evaluating and categorizing organizations according to the types of products that they offer in the marketplace. This will demonstrate that though it may be inappropriate to treat education and soap as equivalent products from a marketing perspective, the tools and concepts of marketing can be applied successfully across a diverse range of product categories, provided the marketer recognizes the special characteristics of each product and its sponsoring organization.

Second, we'll discuss the problems of balancing long-term institutional concerns against short-term customer needs when formulating a marketing strategy. We'll show how the lifetime relationships that colleges seek to form with their major customers, the students, place a premium on understanding and satisfying customer needs as they change over time.

Next, we'll examine what marketing specialists and educational commentators have written about the use of marketing by educational institutions, from both descriptive and normative perspectives. A related issue is how the use of marketing is affecting higher education in the United States.

We'll then discuss unethical marketing practices in higher education and the different forms taken by such abuses. Critics of marketing will probably not be surprised by the length of this section. But they still may be surprised at the wide range of activities that, though included here under the marketing rubric because of their direct impact upon consumers, are frequently perpetrated by individuals who would certainly not perceive themselves as being involved in marketing.

Finally, we shall try to summarize the contributions that a marketing orientation can make to educational institutions, as well as the threats that it poses to the educational system. We'll conclude with some recommendations for minimizing the incidence of abuses and for enhancing the contribution that sound ethical practice of marketing can offer to students, institutions, and the overall system alike.

One cannot, of course, discuss the practice of marketing in higher education without relating it to the broader issue of how marketing tools and concepts are applied in other industries. Similarly, one cannot discuss the applications of marketing to a single management task in higher education (such as recruitment of students to four-year colleges) without reference to the uses and abuses of marketing in other fields of postsecondary education (such as adult education, graduate programs, and proprietary schools) or to other areas of educational management (such as fund raising, alumni activities, management of extracurricular programs).

We believe that this broadened perspective will stimulate a better understanding of the role and limitations of marketing in higher education. In the process we hope to strip away some of the misconceptions surrounding marketing and to enable the thoughtful educational administrator to distinguish the ethically sound practice of marketing from the deliberately or unintentionally abusive, to single out the innovative but appropriate application of marketing tools and concepts from the merely frivolous, and to promote the implementation of cost-effective marketing strategies in place of the simply wasteful.

Is Education a Unique Product?

Educators like to draw attention to what they see as the special, even unique nature of institutions of higher education. Much is made of education's distinctive contributions to the social fabric, of the high-minded ideals to which educators subscribe, of the unusual mission of colleges and universities in nurturing human values and stimulating the intellectual development of society's brightest young minds. The application of marketing techniques to educational institutions, some critics argue, reduces these institutions to the level of cigarette firms and soap manufacturers.

The logical flaw in this argument lies in equating the marketing discipline with the corporate world and with consumer packaged goods in particular. Although it is true that many sophisticated marketing techniques have been developed in and are practiced by consumer-goods companies, the discipline of marketing, with its focus on understanding and facilitating transactions between marketing organizations and their customers, transcends different product categories and sectors of the economy. The challenge for marketing professionals lies in distinguishing between broadly generalizable theoretical notions and the application of specific strategies to specific product situations. For instance, the laws of hydrodynamics provide marine designers with important guidelines for developing steering mechanisms for ships, but no competent naval architect would dream of trying to install the rudder from a supertanker on a Staten Island ferryboat. Similarly, an understanding of economics is helpful to marketers when developing pricing strategies, but the specific pricing strategies used by a soap manufacturer are hardly likely to be an appropriate model for setting college tuition levels and financial aid guidelines.

Towards a Categorization of Products in Marketing

Attempts have been made in the past to distinguish between some of the different types of products that are the subject of marketing efforts. For instance, distinctions have been made between durable goods, nondurable goods, and services; between business and nonbusiness (public and nonprofit) marketing; and between "social marketing" (the marketing of desired behavior patterns) and goods and services marketing. But as Lovelock points out, no unifying conceptual framework has been developed to incorporate each of these categorizations.[2] Accordingly, he proposes the classification scheme shown in Figure 1, which is based upon *who* markets *what* to *whom*, and consists of a three-way matrix comprising:

1. Marketers (business, government, nonprofit)
2. Product offerings (physical goods, services, social behavior)
3. Customers (individuals and families, organizations)

Let's look at each grouping and see where higher education fits in this scheme.

Marketer Characteristics. Each of the three types of marketers — *business, government,* and *nonprofit* — tends to operate with different sets of objectives, receives its revenues from different sources, and is subject to different sets of constraints in planning and implementing marketing strategy. As a generalization, business firms sell products in the marketplace in the expectation that they will not only recoup their financial outlays but also generate a profit. Public and nonprofit organizations, by contrast, often sell their products at prices that are below full cost (and sometimes even give them away), thus requiring attraction of resources through taxes or voluntary donations to cover the resulting financial shortfall.[3] Public agencies are distinguished from private, nonprofit organiza-

35

Figure 1. A Basic Categorization of Market Offerings

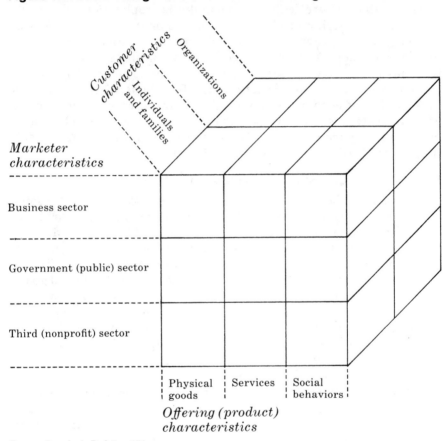

Source: Lovelock, Ref. 2, p. 151.

tions by the constraints of the political arena, which generally include high public visibility and a direct or indirect accountability to elected officials and the public.

Offering Characteristics. The nature of the product offered has a major bearing on how transactions are facilitated and consummated in the marketplace. *Services*, broadly defined, account for close to two-thirds of the U.S. gross national product, which, of course, includes the output of the public and nonprofit sectors. Yet the marketing of services was neglected until recently in favor of *physical goods* such as commodities and manufactured goods.

Bateson and others argue that service marketing raises different problems from those facing marketing managers in goods producing firms.[4]

Kotler and Zaltman coined the term "social marketing" to describe programmatic activities aimed at influencing the acceptability of social ideas and thereby bringing about attitudes and behavior patterns that were congruent with these ideas. As examples, they cited campaigns to promote birth control, charitable giving, safe driving, nonsmoking, civil rights, and pollution control.[5] For clarity, we will use the term *social behaviors* to encompass those individual or group behaviors that collectively have an impact on broader segments of society.

Customer Characteristics. Who the customer is represents an important determinant of how the product is marketed. The buying behavior of *organizations* differs from that of *individuals and families* in several important respects, including the number of individuals involved in making or approving the purchase decision, the size of the typical purchase transaction, and the constraining influence of the organization's need to be run efficiently.

What Sort of Product Is Higher Education?

The great majority of institutions of higher education are either public or nonprofit (although if one includes all institutions of postsecondary education, then the business sector is represented by the numerous proprietary schools).

Education is essentially a service industry. To the extent that colleges and universities attempt to socialize their students to behave in ways that are perceived as benefiting the broader society, they are engaged in social behavior marketing, too. But the core of the educational product consists of services that are consumed directly by students, primarily for their own benefit. This does not mean that they also pay for these services (such payments may be made by parents, other family members, corporate sponsors, or benefactors). Even in situations where an organization commissions and pays for an educational program on behalf of its members or employees, it only benefits to the extent that the individual consumers of the program absorb the material presented to them.

In short, then, the great majority of higher education products are represented by only 2 of the 18 cells depicted in Figure 1:

- A public organization marketing services to individuals
- A nonprofit organization marketing services to individuals

The only parallel with soap or cigarettes lies in the fact that these products are also marketed to individuals. This is hardly a convincing argument for a direct transfer of techniques and strategies!

Characteristics of Public and Nonprofit Organizations

Observers agree that marketing has achieved acceptance among many nonbusiness managers during the past decade. For instance, Lovelock and Weinberg and also Kotler cite a number of success stories in which a marketing orientation has enabled a public or nonprofit organization to achieve improved performance and greater customer satisfaction. However, they also draw attention to the failures that have resulted from rushing into marketing with more enthusiasm than understanding.[6] Many of these failures may be attributed to a misunderstanding of the essential differences between business and nonbusiness marketing.

Public or nonprofit status influences an organization's marketing strategy in a variety of ways, reflecting the distinctive characteristics of such organizations.[7]

First, unlike private firms, public and nonprofit organizations do not seek to maximize profits. Financial performance serves more as a constraint than as an objective for nonbusiness managers. Instead, the aim is to achieve other social, cultural, environmental, or economic benefits that are consistent with the organization's sense of mission. That makes it much harder to define and measure performance.

Even where the organization's products are sold to customers at a price, the resulting revenues are rarely sufficient to cover the full costs. A separate marketing effort is required to obtain the donations or tax revenues needed to cover the resulting deficit. This, in turn, requires a commitment from donors (or legislators and voters) to the mission of the organization. The challenge for nonbusiness managers is to be responsive to changing customer needs without losing the support of donors and others who prefer a traditional interpretation of mission.

Nonbusiness managers must deal with a broader array of constituencies and contend with a higher level of public scrutiny than do most of their business counterparts. The concerns of donor groups (or legislators and voters) tend to have much more impact on day-to-day management actions than do those of stockholders on a company. And whereas stockholders tend to have a common interest in the company's financial performance (although there are exceptions), donors tend to have a range of different and sometimes conflicting concerns, as any college president will testify.

The nonmarket pressures under which nonbusiness managers find themselves are compounded in situations where tax-supported funds are being used to deliver services to a relatively small segment of the population. This may lead to pressures to add new programs that serve a larger segment or else to cut back funding. The problem is further complicated by the fact that adding new services in an effort to appear responsive may dilute the quality of the core product.

Finally, the great majority of nonbusiness organizations market services rather than goods. As will be shown in the next section, the marketing of services requires a different approach to that employed for goods.

Clearly, public and nonprofit organizations do have some distinctive characteristics that influence or constrain the application of marketing tools and strategies. For this reason, college and university administrators would do well to study the marketing efforts of such organizations as hospitals and other health services, public transportation agencies, public broadcasting stations, postal services, museums, and performing arts organizations. They should review the use of marketing for fund raising as well as for developing and delivering services. Since there are still relatively few cases of exemplary marketing programs among public and nonprofit organizations, it may be helpful to review business experience, too. But the most appropriate parallels concern the marketing of services, not goods.

How Do Services Differ from Physical Goods?

In a company that manufactures physical goods there can be considerable (but obviously not total) separation between production and marketing, once agreements on a product line, production scheduling, warehousing, shipping, and related procedures have been reached.

Both marketing theorists and experienced managers agree that services marketing differs from goods marketing and requires a different approach. The following list summarizes some problems in the marketing and utilization of services:[8]

1. Services are created through the interaction of customers, employees, and service facilities. In many service organizations (and education is one of them) the characteristics and behavior of cus-

tomers contribute to or detract from the quality of the product.

2. The finished service is consumed as it is produced. Hence service organizations cannot use inventories for the service portion of the finished product (e.g., chalk and textbook supplies can be kept in a warehouse, but tutorial sessions cannot).

3. Since services cannot be inventoried, economic success in service organizations is often a function of their ability to match customer demand to productive capacity at all times, and thus avoid the "feast or famine" syndrome. Hence the interest of educational institutions in developing evening, weekend, and summer programs.

4. It is much harder to control the quality of services than that of goods. This is, in part, because services can't be inventoried; in part, because services such as education rely heavily on personal interactions that cannot be mass produced on an assembly line.

5. If the service organization wants to grow outside a particular geographic market, it has to develop new "production facilities" in new locations, thus compounding the problem of quality control. This is a particular problem for colleges that operate "branch" or "satellite" campuses.

6. The "mental image" of the service can be "fuzzy," since many components of services are intangible and difficult to describe. Because prospective users may place a premium on the reputation of the organization from which the service is obtained, word-of-mouth recommendations by friends and associates may become very important.

7. It is more difficult for prospective customers to sample a service than it is for them to sample a physical product. One can try a small tube of toothpaste or test-drive a car, but visiting a campus and sitting in on a class is less likely to give a representative experience.

8. Services are highly experiential; whether or not customers are satisfied with a service such as education depends on their reactions to a variety of experiences, ranging from physical facilities such as the classroom or dormitory to personal services such as those provided by the instructor, the registrar, or the librarian.

What does that mean for those engaged in marketing higher education services? Essentially it says, *on balance*, better insights and understanding may be gained from studying the marketing practices of well-run hotels, airlines, and insurance companies than will be gained from looking at those of soap firms, cigarette companies, and automobile manufacturers. The one caveat is that for many service firms marketing is still a relatively new concept; many still adhere to a product or selling concept of management. Therefore, educational managers must be selective in choosing service organizations as models for study.

Level of Consumer Involvement with the Product

In recent years, marketing theorists have begun to distinguish between products that generate a high degree of personal involvement in the purchase decision on the part of the consumer and those that do not.[9] In developing a marketing strategy for an organization, it is important to understand where its products are located on the high-involvement–low-involvement continuum.

Among the factors that influence consumer involvement with a product are the following:

▪ *Cost*—the higher the cost, the greater the risk, and therefore the higher the consumer's involvement.

▪ *Frequency of purchase*—frequent purchases build up greater levels of experience, which, in turn, reduce the need to become highly involved in any single purchase decisions.

▪ *Product complexity*—the more relevant, performance-related characteristics possessed by the product, the higher the consumer's involvement as he or she struggles to evaluate each.

▪ *Similarities of choice*—similar competing alternatives require less involvement on the consumer's part since it is more difficult to make a poor choice and the cost of making a wrong decision is slight.

When we consider these dimensions, it is clear that soap is a low-involvement product and a new car is a high-involvement one. Rothschild[10] generalizes that higher education tends to be a high-involvement product (see Figure 2), implying that college marketers have more to learn from automobile marketers than from packaged-goods marketers. Obviously, the exact location of higher education on the involvement continuum is going to depend on the individual student and on the nature of the educational product itself. Choosing a four-year college education, for instance, is presumably more "involving" than selecting a one-semester extension course, since the former requires a longer time commitment and comprises a much more complex "bundle" of services—including education, food and lodging, recreation, and social activities.

The importance of the involvement concept for marketers lies primarily in the development of appropriate communications strategies. Low-involvement products can be sold largely through ad-

Figure 2. Hypothesized Continuum of Consumer Involvement with Different Types of Products

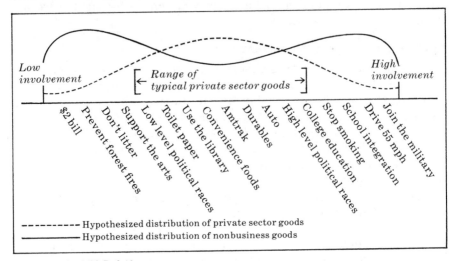

Source: Rothschild, Ref. 10.

vertising—an impersonal communications medium. For high-involvement products, advertising may generate awareness and knowledge, but personal communication (through the medium of salespeople or other personnel) is needed to respond to customer questions and concerns before the sale is actually completed.

A significant conclusion to be drawn from this concept concerns the appropriateness (as opposed to the ethics) of "hard-sell" advertising and promotional gimmicks. The high-involvement nature of the educational product implies that though such efforts may raise awareness among prospective students, they will not of themselves lead students to decide to attend the institution. In short, high-pressure advertising and gimmicky promotions, providing their content is truthful, are probably not putting unfair pressure on prospective students. However, high-pressure personal communications are another matter.

The implication for educational marketers is they will learn more from studying those marketing situations that represent major decisions and involve a mix of both personal and impersonal communications than they will learn from studying soap or cigarette marketing. As a generalization, it is probably true to say that services generate higher involvement than physical goods, because they are less easy to visualize and therefore more difficult to evaluate.

Summary

On the basis of this evaluation, can we say that higher education is a unique product? The answer is a qualified "yes" if we restrict ourselves to the four-year college education. We have already shown that this is a complex, high-involvement, public/nonprofit service. That much it has in common with the products of hospitals and certain arts organizations. It is also a long-lasting product (consumption extends over four years but its benefits usually last a lifetime) that is purchased only once by the majority of consumers. Perhaps enrollment in the armed forces is the closest parallel, but the nature of this experience is rather different and the choices narrower; additionally, the "price" to the military recruit is expressed in terms of time commitment and some loss of personal freedom, rather than financial outlays; one of the benefits of military service is the salary that comes with it.[11]

Does this mean that educational managers have nothing to learn from the marketing of other types of products? Here the answer must be an emphatic no. All the elements of the marketing mix — product development, pricing, communication, and delivery — are present here. There is competition from a wide array of similar colleges. There is a large market of prospective consumers who can be usefully grouped into different segments.

The distinction between higher education and other products lies in how the various tools of marketing are applied. The most direct transfers of marketing technology should come from well-conceived and well-executed programs involving similar types of products. Poorly executed efforts are only useful for the insights they provide in how *not* to proceed. Less closely related products may still provide good insights, but at a higher level of generalization; the specific techniques and strategies employed are probably not transferable to higher education.

One important caveat at this point, however, is that we have been focusing our attention on only one item in the portfolio of products offered by the typical college or university, namely four-year degree programs. Figure 3 lists some of the other areas in higher education to which marketing may be applied. To the several different types of residential degree programs, one must also add extension and continuing education courses, fund raising efforts,

Figure 3. Some Activities in Higher Education Requiring Marketing

1. Recruitment and admission of new students
   - Traditional undergraduate programs
   - Transfers
   - Graduate programs
   - Extension degree programs and courses
   - Continuing education (noncredit)
2. Student retention
3. Placement of graduates
4. Alumni relations
5. Parent relations
6. Community relations
7. Development
   - Annual and capital fund raising
   - Alumni and corporate donors
8. Faculty and staff recruitment and retention
9. Campus programs
   - Athletics
   - Performing arts
10. Other auxiliary services
    - Food services
    - Bookstores
    - Miscellaneous recreational activities
    - Campus housing, etc.

and alumni activities, for which the marketing tasks may often be sharply different. Colleges and universities also offer a wide range of supplementary or auxiliary services, some internally focused, others directed at prospective consumers both on and off campus. Each of these products requires its own marketing program, but each program must be developed with reference to other marketing efforts and an understanding of how it relates to the broad institutional mission.

Balancing Institutional and Customer Needs

Marketing has been described by some as "the science of transaction."[12] Marketplace transactions usually involve exchanges of value between two parties, although in some instances (as is common in higher education), a third party may pay for the product received by the consumer. For a voluntary transaction to take place, each party must feel that fair value is being received at the time the exchange is formalized.

Since most marketing organizations hope to sell their products to a large number of customers, and since many customers periodically need to repurchase the same type of product, an organization's success is clearly dependent upon its ability to satisfy customer needs. But the product must be sold on realistic terms (financial or otherwise) lest the organization find itself unable to generate the resources it needs to remain in operation. Institutions of higher education are no exception, despite the availability (in some instances) of donations and grants to supplement tuition revenues.

This dependency on satisfying customer needs raises a key question: to what extent should a college offer students what *they* want as opposed to providing them with what the institution feels is best? A review of the commercially derived *marketing concept* reveals the financial and ethical dilemmas posed by this question.

The Marketing Concept

Introduced into U.S. business during the 1950s by the General Electric Company, the marketing concept is based on two fundamental notions: First, the consumer is recognized as the focal point or pivot of all business activity; second, profit rather than sales volume is specified as the criterion for evaluating marketing activities, since making financial profits is the private sector firm's main rationale for existence.[13] Essentially, this concept sees an organization's primary function as attempting to satisfy the needs of its customers, provided it is consistent with its mission to do so. This involves developing products that meet consumer needs and then pricing, distributing, and communicating about them in ways that show an understanding of customer characteristics and behavior.

However, not all organizations practice the marketing concept. Some espouse the *product concept*, which leads to production of whatever an organization is competent at producing under the assumption that good products reasonably priced will essentially sell themselves. Others subscribe to the *selling concept,* a management orientation that emphasizes the use of sales and advertising techniques to "push" whatever the organization has produced. Many observers have centered their criticisms of marketing on firms that practice the selling concept by trying to persuade consumers to buy things that the former has produced but the latter don't need.

At first glance, the marketing concept appears both realistic and responsive. But it, too, is now coming under attack. Bennett and Cooper argue that blind adherence to this concept has led to a short-term focus on consumer needs, as expressed by current buying behavior. The net result, they say, has been a decline in the rate of product innovation and a trend towards proliferation of "me-too" products. The danger of such an approach is that the organization becomes preoccupied with the present and overlooks future opportunities to serve customers better.[14]

From the perspective of educational managers, this short-term, reactive perspective leads inevitably to a strategy of catering to current student fads and copying what other, seemingly successful institutions are doing, rather than taking a long-term view of developing educational programs designed to equip students for lifetimes that will extend well into the twenty-first century.

In brief, the challenge for higher education is to remain sensitive to the short-term needs and concerns of students and other constituencies (such as parents and alumni) without undercutting the institution's evaluation of broader societal needs and its own long-term sense of mission. The response to purely market pressures must be tempered by consideration of the skills and concerns of such internal groups as faculty and staff, as well as the constraints and opportunities posed externally by regulators and funding sources.

Maintaining Customer Loyalty

Institutions of higher education, like most commercial marketers, depend for success on their ability not only to attract new customers but also to instill "brand loyalty" among existing ones. In a sense, each time donors make a gift to the annual fund, each time alumni attend a reunion, these individuals are making repeat purchases.

In a marketing context, loyalty is typically a function of a customer's prior experience with the organization and its products. For this reason there is a strong incentive among marketers who are looking for repeat purchases to maintain the quality of their product, serve their customers well, and refrain from any dubious or unethical practices.

One of the unusual characteristics of educational marketing is that colleges and universities typically see the relationship entered into with each new student customer as potentially lasting a lifetime. Educational consumers go through a "life cycle" with their alma mater that is almost as multifaceted as Shakespeare's seven ages of man. From an initial phase as prospects, inquirers, and then applicants, they go on to become admittees, matriculants, and students. After a lapse of some years, they graduate to alumni status, becoming (the institution hopes) loyal donors and volunteers. In time, many become parents of a new generation who may, possibly, go through the same cycle with the same institution.

Figure 4. The Student Life-Cycle:
Changing Marketing Tasks for Changing Roles

Task	*Target*	*Influences*

Recruitment.	Prospect
	Inquirer
	Applicant
		Parents
		Friends
		High school
		   counselors &
		   teachers

Retention	Admittee Matriculant Student	Parents Fellow students Other friends
Career Development.	Match Graduating student to Prospective employers and Graduate schools	Faculty Counselors Fellow students Employers Graduate schools Family & friends
Fund Raising and **Voluntarism**	Alumnus/alumna . . . . . Donor/volunteer. . . . . . Parent	Fellow alumni Spouses Peer groups Children?

As suggested in Figure 4, the marketing task at each stage is different, as are the concerns of the target customer and the influences that are brought to bear on his or her decision. A breakdown in the process at any one point may jeopardize all future relationships with the individual in question. Thus a prospective student who passes the screening process but is displeased at the way his application has been handled may elect to go elsewhere. A student who perceives the quality of the education she is receiving to be inferior to that promised may transfer out. An alumnus who is aggrieved at his alma mater because he feels that the placement office made no attempt to help him find a job may refuse to respond to fund-raising appeals. And donors or volunteers who believe that their efforts on the part of the college have gone unappreciated may encourage their children to apply elsewhere. Among private colleges, especially, economic survival is dependent on developing and continually adding to a large pool of generous contributors. This potential resource may be jeopardized in the long run if the institution fails in its relationships with its student customers.

As in many marketing situations, the impact of good or poor treatment of customers may be compounded by the power of word-of-mouth advertising. Customers who are particularly pleased with, or dissatisfied by, their experiences with a particular product may share their opinions with friends and associates, thus influencing their behavior, too. This is particularly likely in the case of a high-involvement product like education that is also of broad general interest.

But there is a further twist in higher education. Students are not only consumers of educational services. They are also changed by that experience and themselves become a product of the institution in the eyes of third parties such as employers, graduate schools, donors, and prospective students.[15] Poor selection procedures at a particular college, delivery of education that is perceived as weak by these third parties, or, even worse, a combination of both failings will mean that the institution's graduates will not be well regarded. The reverse, of course, is also true.

How Is Marketing Being Used in Higher Education?

A review of some of the published literature on marketing in higher education not only provides good insights into developments in this field during the 1970s but also clarifies the breadth of the marketing function and the need for senior college administrators to become involved in marketing decision making for their institutions.

The first published use of the term *marketing* in the context of an article on higher education was by Krachenberg. Emphasizing that a number of management techniques were being adopted by colleges and universities, but that the potential of marketing remained unappreciated, he went on to identify the benefits of marketing analysis, tools, and strategies. He also spoke bluntly of the antagonism aroused by marketing:

"Unfortunately, to many people the term marketing has a less than positive connotation. It has become a catch-word standing for all the undesirable elements in American business: the foisting of worthless products on an unsuspecting public; the aggressiveness of Madison Avenue and its immoral manipulation of people. In short, marketing is looked upon by many as being fundamentally self-seeking and thus unacceptable by its very nature....

"[However, if] anything is undesirable about marketing, it is not in the activity per se; rather it is in the motives of those guiding the activity and the manner in which it is carried out."[16]

Earlier there had been articles on innovative or improved practices in admissions[17] or on educational fund raising. But Krachenberg's article marked the beginning of attempts to gain better understanding of how marketing could be applied in managing educational institutions. For instance, Gorman focused on marketing's role in promoting student enrollments, emphasizing the need for an institution to review its resources and to promote its "differential advantages" to those market segments most likely to be receptive to them.[18] Buchanan and Barksdale turned the marketing spotlight on continuing education and university extension; after surveying 90 extension educators on practices at their schools, they concluded that extension service units were performing marketing-like activities using a variety of marketing management tools "whether or not they are recognized as such."[19]

Refining the Use of Marketing in Higher Education

Two perceptive and thought-provoking papers on marketing appeared during 1975 in the journal *Liberal Education*. Ihlanfeldt discussed the application of marketing techniques to tackling the problem of declining enrollments. He stressed that such efforts could not be confined to admissions: "I do not believe that improving the marketing techniques in the admission operation is the answer to the problem of declining enrollments if a high rate of attrition shows that a school is not meeting the needs of its current students."[20] In short, educators should patch the holes in the bucket before asking admissions to pump more water into it.

Ihlanfeldt also drew a distinction between staying abreast of consumer needs and pandering to fads:

"As a service industry trying to serve a declining market or a changing market, there must be a tolerance for such terms as program modification, program development, and consumerism. We are all in the business of attempting to accommodate the needs of various student constituencies and at times this requires program modifications as well as new program development. We are not unlike a profit-making corporation that is constantly reviewing the demand for present products and investigating possible new products. The admission or marketing officer has the responsibility of assessing consumer needs and translating those needs back to the community for consideration. This does not imply that an institution must respond to every demand or fad that exists in the marketplace. To the contrary, only by staying abreast of the capricious nature of the marketplace can the institution make decisions of a noncapricious nature."[21]

Ihlanfeldt's view of the nature and role of communications was equally perceptive:

"The communication responsibility can be divided into an internal and external process. The internal function is to communicate effectively and persuasively [within the institution] the needs of the marketplace. The external function is to communicate effectively to the consumer what the institution has to offer."[22]

He concluded by emphasizing that it is the *faculty*, not the admissions office, that creates the educational product — admissions is limited to communicating the strengths of that product to student consumers and their families.

The second paper, by Hugstad, sought to show "why some, but not all, of the marketing methods used in business can be transferred to serve the ends of higher education." Central to Hugstad's thesis was the argument that there were significant differences in goals and operating climate between the corporate and educational structures. In particular, he argued that universities had been too oriented to the short-run goal of organizational survival; instead they should be asking how they could better serve society's needs. "The questions being asked," he wrote, "appear to be closer to those asked by industry, namely, 'Where is the market?' rather than 'who should be the market?'"[23] But his insinuation that corporations use marketing as a short-term tool to dig themselves out of temporary difficulties strikes us as an unrealistic depiction of corporate reality: the most successful firms tend to be those that periodically reevaluate their long-term direction from a marketing perspective and redirect their efforts accordingly.

Hugstad was closer to the mark when stating that personal selling and advertising were "the marketing techniques most visibly borrowed by educational administrators." He criticized the common failure to distinguish between the "two vital promotional functions" of (1) information dissemination and (2) persuasion, noting that the first had an important role to play but many found the use of persuasive techniques repugnant in educational institutions. He went on to suggest that educators needed to develop a better understanding of the role of pricing and distribution in influencing demand, arguing that good insights could be gained in these areas from studying business marketing.

Perhaps his major concern centered on the consequences of applying the marketing concept to higher education:

"The marketing concept, as currently practiced by most businesses, is a short-run concept, emphasizing the basic need to give people what they want, which may or may not be consistent with the larger, long-range question of what they need."

Thus, he criticized pressures to make higher education programs more appealing to students, lest this result in undermining the quality and long-term value of the academic product.[24]

At a colloquium on college admissions sponsored by the College Board in 1976, Kotler provided some pungent examples of "excessive and misguided" attempts to increase enrollment that smacked more of hard selling than marketing. Like Ihlanfeldt, he also sought to clarify the restricted role of the admissions office:

"It is a widespread misperception among college administrators that the college marketing process is the responsibility of the admissions office....

"The marketing work of a college does not begin in the admissions office but in the offices of the president and the board of trustees. The college's top policymakers must articulate a mission and purpose for the college that makes sense in the light of its history, resources, opportunities, and competition.... It should define a distinct posture of the college relative to other colleges."[25]

Kotler went on to point out that the "student drawing power" of a college depended on the number and kinds of programs offered by that institution, or what he termed its "portfolio." In addition to a range of different academic programs, he noted that "The college's overall portfolio also consists of other 'consumerable' aspects of that institution, such as a distinguished lecture series, concert and drama programs, an active student union, and so on."[26]

Using the tools of consumer analysis, Kotler also showed how an understanding of the student decision process in college applications could help admissions offices in developing appropriate strategies for attracting applicants who were well matched to the institution.[27]

The issue of developing a distinctive institutional posture was picked up at the same colloquium by Geltzer and Ries. These authors, principals of a public relations firm, discussed how a college might use consumer research to develop a communications strategy that would emphasize those of its strong points that were important to prospects. They cited numerous examples of "positioning" strategies used by companies or products in the private sector to demonstrate the importance of an institution's promoting attributes that were both relevant to customers and distinctive relative to competitors.[28]

Subsequent articles on educational marketing have become increasingly specific. Leister and MacLachlan demonstrated how market segmentation analysis could be used to help a four-year college assess the community college transfer market.[29] Building on earlier work by Kotler,[30] Berry and Allen looked at how an institution could develop successful exchange relationships with the numerous different "publics" with which it must interact — current and prospective students, alumni, donors, parents, counselors, accrediting agencies, community organizations, faculty and staff, the media, and many others.[31] Both these authors and Sussman[32] demonstrated the need for colleges to develop an institution-wide marketing organization, integrating the marketing functions of admissions, public relations, development, and alumni relations through a policy of placing them all under a single vice president, who would report directly to the college president.

How Is the Use of Marketing Affecting Higher Education?

From asking how marketing tools and strategies are being used in higher education, it is a short and logical step to ask what effect the practice of marketing is having on educational institutions and the "industry" in general.

Consumer Protection in Higher Education

Paralleling the growing consumerism of the seventies in the private sector has been increased concern for the rights of consumers in higher education. In a keynote address at a conference on consumer protection in postsecondary education, Congresswoman Patricia Schroeder discussed 25 possible consumer concerns identified by the U.S. Office of Education.[33] Willett examined these concerns in more depth and considered how best to protect consumers against such abuses.[34]

Echoing a theme raised earlier in a legal discussion by Peterson,[35] Bender asked, "Can your catalogue stand the test of FTC guidelines?"[36] El-Khawas demonstrated ways in which colleges might respond to consumerism issues by citing examples of good practice. She emphasized the need to avoid deliberately or inadvertently misleading students in advance of enrollment and to treat them fairly once enrolled.[37]

Most recently, the Carnegie Council has enlarged upon these previous discussions and emphasized that ethical behavior in higher education is a two-way street: students have responsibilities to their institutions as well as vice versa.[38] Later in this paper, we will discuss some of the council's conclusions concerning marketing abuses by colleges.

Marketing's Impact on Higher Education

Apart from concerns as to the ethics and legality of certain marketing practices (and the need to protect consumers from these), some commentators have also become worried by the impact of marketing activities on the character of higher education itself.

Trachtenberg and Levy expressed anxiety that financially strapped colleges, desperate for new students, might have effectively abandoned all admissions criteria save ability to pay.[39] Fiske described how many colleges had hired consultants to advise them on curriculum changes, communications strategy, and recruitment policies; some had even allowed a consultant to "take over the admissions office."[40]

Business Week and Ricklefs reported moves on the part of many schools to offer more vocationally oriented courses and to add or extend part-time programs in an effort to increase tuition revenues.[41] Recognizing that demand was growing for part-time degree programs among mature adults, Sawhill worried that the competition for these new students was leading to questionable courses and "disreputable" credit-granting practices. "Higher education," he observed tartly, "is approaching the territory of lifelong learning with standards, forethought, and a sense of dignity reminiscent of the California Gold Rush."[42]

Middleton, Kotler, and Fiske have all described some of the attention-getting schemes devised by some institutions to stimulate interest among prospective applicants. The approaches employed (or at least proposed) have included such efforts as distribution of monogrammed Frisbees or besloganed T-shirts, release of balloons containing scholarship offers, and sponsorship of juggling acts in shopping centers.[43]

Predictably, charges of academic hucksterism abound. But is there necessarily anything unethical in all this? It is our contention that from a consumer standpoint there is nothing *morally* wrong in strategies that serve merely to generate awareness of the institution, so long as they do not willfully misrepresent facts in the process. Some of the approaches used represent light-hearted innovations that attract attention and perhaps serve to diminish the stodgy, sanctimonious impression that some people have of college administrators. Others, however, simply make the institutions look foolish and may even discourage applicants. One of the tasks for observers of the educational scene is to learn to distinguish the innovative from the inappropriate, and the unethical from the merely foolish. Let us now examine in depth the issue of unethical practices in educational marketing.

Marketing Abuses in Higher Education

In line with the mistaken notion that marketing is just another name for advertising and sales is the tendency to look at marketing abuses in higher education in terms of false or misleading advertising, or unreasonable pressure by college recruiters on students to enroll. As will be shown, unethical communications are in fact the mechanism that makes possible the real abuses in the product and pricing elements of the marketing mix.

This communications view of marketing is, in certain respects, a deceptively comfortable one for colleges to adopt. It implies that the abuses lie not only outside the faculty but also on the periphery of the administration itself. The blame for abuses can be conveniently shifted to "semi-professionals" outside the mainstream of institutional life who bring tainted values with them and can be quickly excised from the organization if they cause it any problems.

However, it should be recalled that market transactions between a service enterprise and its customers involve four key elements: the product, the delivery systems employed to bring it to the customer, how it is priced (and payment made), and how it is communicated to prospective purchasers. Since these transactions involve both faculty and administrators, the ethical and managerial aspects of marketing abuses are brought to center stage, and the collective decision-making procedure of academic faculties implies a shared responsibility for many such abuses.

Our review in this section will draw heavily from the Carnegie Council's report but will be supplemented by additional insights from other sources.

"Product" Issues

The Carnegie Council's report lists "16 basic rights and responsibilities" of institutions in the area of academic planning, the heart of the higher education product.[44] A number of these responsibilities center on the quality of the programs offered.

In a recent editorial critique of extension education, the *New York Times* stated bluntly: "Like most enterprises, education is a business; one no less likely than any other to offer shoddy merchandise if that will keep the money coming in."[45] That observation could have applied to many conventional, residential degree programs, too.

There are, in a sense, two basic types of "product"abuses. The first represents deviations from the average consumer's fair and reasonable expectations of basic product characteristics. Just as public transportation is expected to meet reasonable standards of safety, so colleges are expected to set reasonable standards of educational quality before awarding degree credits. There may be a benefit to an individual student in letting academic standards slip, but when it is widespread, this practice abuses both present and former students (who may see their own degrees devalued) as well as graduate schools or employers who may find themselves buying a pig in a poke. Other basic attributes that any student has a right to expect include minimum standards of safety, comfort, and hygiene in the institution's physical facilities and food services.

One class of abuses that has received increasing discussion in recent years is the award of certificates, degrees, or diplomas based upon payment of fees rather than educational accomplishment.

Among its manifestations are degree and diploma mills that don't even pretend to require any educational accomplishments in return for the sale of an impressive-looking sheepskin.[46] Legal action has succeeded in closing several such establishments, and some of their operators have been charged with fraud. However, the granting of experiential credits – or what critics have termed "college credits for living"[47] – is perhaps even more pernicious because it fools the purchasers as well as employers (and others) who accept the credits thus awarded at face value. It is also far more pervasive, harder to identify, and probably cannot be eradicated through recourse to the law. The ethical implications of experiential credits were bluntly stated by Norman H. Sam of Lehigh University. In a comment quoted in *U.S. News & World Report,* he said: "There is a flimflam scheme going on in academia, a merchandising of meaningless credit, providing degree candidates with little new learning at exorbitant cost. It is a prostitution of American educational values to take tuition money without offering instruction in return."[48]

This comment suggests that there are two ethical issues related to experiential credits. One involves a devaluation of other people's hard-earned degrees; the other, a failure to deliver value in return for the price paid. In theory, the only justifiable financial charge that might be made for experiential credits is a small administrative one to cover the costs of reviewing the student's past experience and recording credits with the registrar; in practice, the student has been misled into believing that it is the academic legitimization provided by conferment of credit units that counts, rather than the underlying educational process. In short, it is masquerading as education.

The second category of product abuses is tied into communications in that it concerns provision of a product different or inferior from what students were led to expect. Such abuses may include the following:

■ Delivery of instruction programs that are different in content or standards from those promised in the institution's published or verbal communications.

■ Teaching of courses by faculty who are inferior teachers or who fail to live up to their responsibilities in meeting with students outside class and providing adequate feedback on performance. The extensive use of graduate students as teaching assistants must be included here also.

- Failure to provide adequate, effective counseling.
- Failure to provide support services (libraries, laboratories, student accommodations, meals, health services, athletic facilities, etc.) of the promised quality.

Several of these abuses have been particularly prevalent in branch campuses or "distance education" programs.[49] They will be discussed in further detail under the following section on service delivery.

Service Delivery Issues

In addition to those characteristics of the educational product that are central to the benefits anticipated by the purchaser, the way in which the product is actually delivered to students may offer legitimate grounds for discontent.

Students have a right to expect that classes and other educational services will be delivered at the times and in the locations scheduled. Switching hours and locations without warning is unethical if there are no extenuating circumstances and students are thereby deprived of some of the education for which they have paid.

College classrooms and related facilities are, in a sense, the "retail outlets" in which the educational product is delivered. Just as a dirty, drafty, or uncomfortable theater can spoil an otherwise excellent film, so may poor facilities detract from the educational experience. Inevitably, there is some variation in the quality of facilities between colleges and also within colleges. But when there is a consistent pattern of discrimination against certain students enrolled in the institution and paying the same tuition, then one can argue that an abuse is being perpetrated.

That is a particular problem in satellite campuses where the facilities at the local branch may be far inferior to those of the main campus, as manifested in such shortcomings as poor classrooms, minimal or nonexistent libraries, lack of proper catering or recreational facilities, and inadequate or nonexistent student services in the areas of counseling, job placement, or extracurricular activities. These shortcomings may be compounded by product-related deficiencies; for example, the assignment of inferior adjunct faculty.

Delivering educational programs outside an institution's main campus is criticized more and more frequently today. Andrews disparages the practice as "academic colonialism."[50] Moreover, off-campus centers are often not even confined to satellite branches within the same metropolitan area. Reports the *New York Times:*

"The nation's colleges and universities are barreling across the country establishing off-campus centers in the manner of an academic McDonald's setting up hamburger franchises." Part of the problem, says the *Times*, is that "a college licensed and accredited in one place is able to convert that imprimatur into what amounts to automatic approval to operate in other states."[51]

As noted in the same story by an official of the Florida Department of Education, "one of the problems is that the diploma only carries the name of the university and it does not tell that the degree was granted through some branch." But administrators of colleges offering such programs defend the practice. One even went so far as to draw a parallel between higher education and the automobile industry:

"'If there can be a Michigan corporation called General Motors selling its automobiles in 50 states, then why can't there be a free flow of the product we represent?' asked William M. Birenbaum, the president of Antioch, which has been awarding bachelor's and master's degrees in 14 states. . . .'"[52]

The point that Mr. Birenbaum misses is one that we have emphasized throughout this paper. Higher education is not a manufactured product, it is a service. Ordinarily those services that are regulated and that cross state lines either will find themselves regulated by an appropriate agency in each state, or they will be regulated wherever they operate by a federal agency (such as the Civil Aeronautics Board or the Interstate Commerce Commission). Yet out-of-state branch campuses are not covered by any such regulatory body.

Another difference between marketing manufactured goods and services is that the former are typically produced in a limited number of locations (such as an automobile factory), subjected there to quality control procedures, and then shipped to various retail locations for sale to the customer. The finished *service*, by contrast, is produced and consumed at the same location. In a pungent phrase, Levitt describes service outlets as "factories in the field."[53]

The problems of definition and consistency are further compounded when a college delegates at least part of its control over the educational product to educational brokers.[54] These intermediaries — perhaps one should call them franchisees — are profit-making companies that offer, for a fee, to provide specialized off-campus programs on behalf of a sponsoring college.

Pricing Issues

The Carnegie Council lists 10 student rights and institutional responsibilities in the area of financial aid and tuition—the pricing element of higher education's marketing mix.[55] As with the other elements, the abuses are of two types—improper practices per se and failure to honor previously stated policies. In the former category are such ethically questionable practices as the following:

- Failure to identify all program-related costs (e.g., books, laboratory charges, parking, mandatory athletic fees) that may add substantially to the basic board and tuition charges.
- Failure to deliver educational (or other) services in return for fees paid.
- Insufficient refund policies in the event of either institutional cancellations or student withdrawals.
- Failure to inform all students of the availability of loans or scholarships and other price discounts for which they might be eligible.

The second category includes the following abuses:

- Failure to live up to stated refund policies.
- Failure to offer the loans and scholarships advertised.
- Inadequate warning of changes in stated policies (e.g., a sudden hike in tuition, a cut in financial aid, or the introduction of charges for previously free supplementary services).

Perhaps the most glaring of these abuses lies in the area of refund policies. Proprietary schools have been particularly singled out for criticism in this respect,[56] but the Carnegie Council reports that degree-granting institutions have been delinquent, too.[57]

Communication Issues

Misleading advertising, "small-print" contracts, and false promises by high-pressure sales personnel have long been favorite targets of business critics. But thoughtful consumer organizations and regulatory bodies such as the Federal Trade Commission go further in their search for misleading or fraudulent marketing communications. Instruction books, prospectuses, labels, packaging, and retail displays also have the potential to mislead prospective consumers (either wittingly or unwittingly) and are appropriate objects for careful scrutiny.

In the case of college recruiting—whether it be for a degree program at the undergraduate level, an extension course for credits, or a noncredit seminar—there are several communication tools available to an institution. They include print, broadcast, and outdoor advertising; films, recordings, and slide shows; view books, published brochures, catalogs, and leaflets; booths at college fairs; internally and externally distributed periodicals; and information provided by college personnel (or their representatives) by mail or telephone, or in person.

But many of these communication tools are also useful to the institution as it seeks to ensure retention of currently registered students who are in good academic standing. Students need information to make decisions about which courses to enroll in, which types of financial aid to apply for, which extracurricular activities to participate in, which types of jobs to seek through the placement office, and even whether or not to transfer out of the institution. False or misleading communications directed by an institution at current students may raise questions about unethical practice of what might be termed *internal* marketing efforts.

The major classes of abuses falling under the rubric of communications come under two broad headings:

1. *Impersonal communications* through the medium of printed or audiovisual materials whose contents make false promises, present out-of-date facts, distort or otherwise misrepresent the facts, are guilty of selective omissions, or are not comprehensible to inexperienced consumers.

2. *Personal communications* by college employees (or other parties formally representing an institution) who are guilty of any of the abuses noted under (1) above or also apply unfair pressure to achieve the desired behavior on the part of a student or applicant; fail to counsel a student or applicant objectively in a manner that recognizes that individual's own best interests; or fail to respond adequately and honestly to questions asked by a student or applicant.

The Carnegie Council report lists a number of omissions that were found in a 1975 study of catalogs from 210 representative four-year colleges and universities. It also presents the contents of the Barat College prospectus as a model of honestly presented information about a college.[58]

Not only the printed word lies or distorts; photography can also misrepresent reality. Carefully posed photographs that purport to show a "typical" campus scene or selective retouching of negatives can create an image that bears little resemblance to fact. Examples range from the proprietary school in Boston that retouched a photograph of its classroom building to eliminate the Dunkin' Donuts restaurant adjoining the street-level entrance, to the Indiana college whose catalog featured a young couple strolling past a waterfall that was nowhere near the campus.[59] Subtler and more widespread distortions are perpetuated by such practices as including in the catalog numerous pictures of minority students (when there are really few such students at the institution), or showing undergraduates talking in small seminars when these are virtually nonexistent or working with laboratory equipment that would not ordinarily be available to them.[60]

Recruiters using high-pressure sales techniques appear commonly in stories of ruthless proprietary schools,[61] but there is reason to believe that many administrators and faculty members in traditional colleges and universities are also misrepresenting, to both prospective and current students, the products offered by their institutions, the prices charged, and the quality of the facilities in which these services are delivered. This type of misrepresentation is hard to pin down since so much of it takes place in one-on-one communications; moreover, not all of it is deliberate. Yet collectively it adds up to deceptive selling.

Evaluation and Conclusion

The nature of higher education is changing. Old markets, such as the full-time education of 18- to 22-year-old undergraduates, are shrinking. New markets, such as part-time degree courses and continuing education programs for mature adults, are expanding. This situation raises some important ethical and strategic issues for educational marketers.

Traditional Programs

In a declining market, such as that for a traditional four-year college education, where overall demand for the product is falling, an institution that limits its activities to this market must obtain a larger market share just to maintain its present enrollments. To do this, the college must stimulate "selective demand" for its own offerings by promoting these as superior to the competition.

In the short run, colleges that are quick to adopt a marketing orientation should enjoy an initial advantage. Yet for all but the strongest institutions this advantage is likely to be lost as their competitors adopt similar strategies. Philip Kotler's views of the probable scenario were reported in an interview in the *Chronicle of Higher Education:*

"Mr. Kotler predicts that falling enrollments and financial demands will force more and more colleges to practice marketing techniques in the near future.

"In fact, he says, higher education will eventually move into a phase of 'over-marketing,' in which all the untapped sources of students will have been tapped and the colleges will be waging heated battles for a share of the student market. . . .

"Once the student shortage becomes a problem throughout the country, according to Mr. Kotler, higher education will be forced to develop a code of ethics for admissions policies."[62]

We believe that the time for such action is already here, since the pressures on institutions to compromise their standards have never been greater. As we have shown, the standards in question extend far beyond the admissions office. This is true not only for traditional four-year programs but also for many graduate programs, too. The Carnegie Council recommends that regional accrediting associations should "develop and enforce general codes of ethical academic conduct," and that individual colleges and universities should "develop on each campus a code of rights and responsibilities for community members" and "voluntarily work to eliminate institutional irresponsibility."[63] We concur, believing that outside pressure is needed in addition to self-regulation.

Institutional Closure

Fiske argues that as the demand for traditional forms of higher education contracts, so too should the supply: "The fact is that, in a time when there will be a quarter fewer eighteen-year-olds, some colleges *should* fold."[64] Unfortunately, few institutions are willing or able to plan for such a future.

Most of the private colleges that close do so only after they have lost control of the situation; the consequences for their students, faculty, and staff are often severe. Since market factors make it almost inevitable that a number of closures will occur during the next decade, the educational industry should take collective responsibility for seeing that these events are handled in a controlled and dignified fashion. Appropriate steps for the industry as a whole might include setting up a fund to ensure that no college was forced to close in mid-semester and establishment of task forces to assist an institution with all the human, academic, legal, and financial aspects of planning for closure.

Public institutions are in a better position to obtain emergency funding, but some critics charge that political pressure has saved institutions that should rightfully have been closed because of insufficient demand for educational services in a particular geographic area. It is, of course, easier to develop a broad regional view of supply-and-demand imbalances where state or community institutions are concerned. Perhaps the national trend toward imposing spending limits on state and local governments will make it politically easier to implement necessary closures of public campuses.

Continuing Education

The growing demand for continuing education offers many colleges the opportunity to diversify their product portfolios by introducing or expanding offerings in this area.[65] This increased demand is particularly strong among older adults.[66] In response, a number of exciting innovations have been introduced. Some like Britain's Open University have focused on new delivery systems to bring higher education to those who might find it too inconvenient to be able to enroll in traditional institutions.[67] Little and Gilliland describe a similar American innovation.[68] New courses and programs have also been developed. But it is clear from the remarks of Sawhill and others that all is not well in the growing field of adult education.[69] There are two reasons for this conclusion, both of which are related to marketing.

The first concerns what private-sector marketers would call "product-company fit." The fact that an organization is good at producing and marketing one type of good or service does not mean it can automatically expect to be successful with another, different product. This issue is well illustrated by the problems encountered by the University of Bridgeport in developing a continuing education program.

"The university found that the road wasn't as smooth as it looked. It took more people to handle admissions for continuing education students than to process full-time students, and the diverse new adult population could not be handled as easily as its relatively homogeneous undergraduate counterpart. Unexpected competition arose in the form of a lower-priced (and lower-quality) program at a nearby institution.

"Bridgeport soon found that it was filling seats but losing money.

'It takes six part-time students to bring in the same cash flow as one full-time student,' said . . . the University's president. 'We woke up to that belatedly.'"[70]

The moral here is that, even within a single institution, marketing strategies have to be adapted to fit the specific characteristics of the product and its target customers.

The second issue concerns an organization's mission. A nonprofit educational institution's primary objectives are not financial ones, since its mission (unlike that of a business firm) is not to make profits. For educational managers concerned with delivery of educational services (as opposed to fund raising), financial matters are an important *constraint* on the organization's ability to achieve its objectives, but they are not the target of those objectives. Unfortunately, continuing education programs are often developed specifically with profits in mind.

When the objective for one of the organization's products is seen as profits, but the objective of another closely related product is quite different, a serious potential for confusion and conflict results. This confusion may also extend to the organization's various constituencies. As nonprofit colleges and universities add more and more vocationally oriented courses, they must recognize they are competing more and more closely with proprietary schools. It would not be surprising if both consumers and regulatory agencies started seeing the two groups as equivalent units.

Conclusion

Marketing is a fact of life in American higher education. Like Molière's character Monsieur Jourdain, who discovered to his amazement that he had been speaking prose for 40 years without being aware of this, administrators at some of the better-run and more responsive institutions have been surprised to find that they have, in fact, been practicing marketing without realizing it. On the other hand, some of those who claim to be marketing oriented are actually abusing or misusing certain marketing tools to engage in activities ranging from high-pressure selling to silly promotional stunts.

Critics should recognize that the technology of marketing is neutral; what they should be worried about is how educational managers are using marketing concepts, tools, and strategies in their institutions. Marketing research and analysis can be employed to gain a better understanding of current and prospective students, and of an institution's ability to serve their needs in an increasingly competitive environment. This understanding can be used to develop strategies that are ethical or unethical. A lack of such understanding will probably result in strategies that are administratively foolish rather than managerially sound.

The issue is not, *should* marketing be used in managing institutions of higher education, but *how* can it be best employed? Answering the latter question requires a clear understanding of the nature and role of the marketing discipline as it applies to public and nonprofit service organizations rather than to manufacturers of packaged consumer goods.

We believe that higher education in general stands to benefit from a stronger marketing orientation. The challenge for the industry is to ensure that ethical standards are maintained and that short-term expediency does not win out over long-term planning.

References

1. Bart Barnes, "Hood: Women's College Stays Just That, but Shifts Image," *Washington Post*, August 9, 1974, pp. D1, D16. Liz Roman Gallese, "New Image: The Women's Colleges Have Bounced Back, Changing Emphasis," *Wall Street Journal*, November 14, 1974, pp. 1, 33.

2. Christopher H. Lovelock, "Theoretical Contributions from Services and Nonbusiness Marketing," pp. 147-165 in *Conceptual and Theoretical Developments in Marketing*, O. C. Ferrell, S. W. Brown, and C. W. Lamb, editors. Chicago: American Marketing Association, 1979.

3. Benson P. Shapiro, "Marketing for Nonprofit Organizations," *Harvard Business Review*, Vol. 51, September-October 1973, pp. 123-132.

4. John E. G. Bateson, "Why We Need Services Marketing," pp. 131-146 in *Conceptual and Theoretical Developments*, Ferrell et al.

5. Philip Kotler and Gerald Zaltman, "Social Marketing: An Approach to Planned Social Change," *Journal of Marketing*, Vol. 35, July 1971, pp. 3-12.

6. Christopher H. Lovelock and Charles B. Weinberg, "Public and Nonprofit Marketing Comes of Age," pp. 413-452 in *Review of Marketing 1978*, G. Zaltman and T. Bonoma, editors. Chicago: American Marketing Association, 1978. Philip Kotler, "Strategies for Introducing Marketing into Nonprofit Organizations," *Journal of Marketing*, Vol. 43, Winter 1979, pp. 37-44.

7. Christopher H. Lovelock and Charles B. Weinberg, "Contrasting Private and Public Sector Marketing," pp. 242-247 in *Marketing's Contributions to the Firm and to Society*, R. C. Curhan, editor. Chicago: American Marketing Association, 1975. Lovelock and Weinberg, "Public and Nonprofit Marketing."

8. Abstracted from Pierre Eiglier, Eric Langeard, Christopher Lovelock, John Bateson, and Robert Young, "Marketing Consumer Services: New Insights." Cam-

bridge, Mass.: Marketing Science Institute, 1977. And *Advertising Age*, Series on Marketing and the Services Industry: "Greater Marketing Emphasis by Holiday Inn Breaks Mold," January 15, 1979, pp. 47-50; "Listening to Consumer Is Key to Consumer or Service Marketing," February 19, 1979, pp. 54-60; "Financial Service Marketers Must Learn Packaged Goods Selling Tools," March 19, 1979, pp. 58-62; "Service Business Is People Dealing with Other People," May 15, 1979, pp. 57-58.

9. Michael J. Houston and Michael L. Rothschild, "A Paradigm for Research on Consumer Involvement." Working Paper 12-77-46, University of Wisconsin-Madison, 1978.

10. Michael L. Rothschild, "Marketing Communications in Nonbusiness Situations or Why It's So Hard to Sell Brotherhood like Soap," *Journal of Marketing*, Vol. 43, Spring 1979, pp. 11-20.

11. A. J. Martin, "Marketing's Application to the Volunteer Military," *Journal of Marketing*, Vol. 43, Fall 1979, pp. 133-134.

12. Shelby D. Hunt, "The Nature and Scope of Marketing," *Journal of Marketing*, Vol. 40, July 1976, pp. 17-28.

13. Hiram C. Barksdale and Bill Darden, "Marketers' Attitudes toward the Marketing Concept," *Journal of Marketing*, Vol. 35, October 1971, pp. 29-36. In the case of public and nonprofit organizations, where financial performance is typically a constraint rather than a primary goal, the organization's nonfinancial goals, as articulated in its mission statement, became its raison d'être.

14. Roger C. Bennett and Robert G. Cooper, "Beyond the Marketing Concept," *Business Horizons*, June 1979, pp. 76-83.

15. Larry Litten, "Marketing Higher Education: Benefits and Risks for the American Academic System," *Journal of Higher Education*, Vol. LI, January 1980, pp. 40-59.

16. A. R. Krachenberg, "Bringing the Concept of Marketing to Higher Education," *Journal of Higher Education*, Vol. XLIII, May 1972, p. 380.

17. B. Alden Thresher, *College Admissions and the Public Interest.* New York: College Entrance Examination Board, 1966. L. Richard Meeth, "Innovative Admissions Practices for the Liberal Arts College," *Journal of Higher Education*, Vol. XLI, October 1970, pp. 535-546.

18. Walter P. Gorman, "Marketing Approaches for Promoting Student Enrollment in Higher Educational Administrations," *College and University*, Vol. 49, Spring 1974, pp. 242-250.

19. W. Wray Buchanan and H. C. Barksdale, "Marketing's Broadening Concept is Real in University Extension," *Adult Education*, Vol. XXV, No. 1, 1974, pp. 34-46.

20. William Ihlanfeldt, "A Management Approach to the Buyer's Market," *Liberal Education*, May 1975, p. 136.

21. Ibid., p. 137.

22. Ibid., p. 141.

23. Paul S. Hugstad, "The Marketing Concept in Higher Education," *Liberal Education*, December 1975, p. 506.

24. Ibid., p. 510.

25. Philip Kotler, "Applying Marketing Theory to College Admissions," pp. 55-57 in

A Role for Marketing in College Admissions. New York: College Entrance Examination Board, 1976.

26. Ibid., p. 59.

27. Ibid., pp. 60-62.

28. Howard Geltzer and Al Ries, "The Positioning Era: A Marketing Strategy for College Admissions in the 1980s," pp. 73-85 in *Role for Marketing.*

29. Douglas V. Leister and Douglas L. MacLachlan, "Assessing the Community College Transfer Market," *Journal of Higher Education,* Vol. XLVII, November/December 1976, pp. 661-680.

30. Philip Kotler, *Marketing for Nonprofit Organizations.* Englewood Cliffs, N.J.: Prentice-Hall, Inc., 1975.

31. Leonard L. Berry and Bruce H. Allen, "Marketing's Crucial Role for Institutions of Higher Education," *Atlanta Economic Review,* July/August 1977, pp. 24-31.

32. Gerald Sussman, "Views of Administrators in Higher Education Regarding the Extent and Adequacy of the Marketing Activities Performed by Their Organizations." Ph. D. dissertation, Boston College, 1979.

33. Patricia Schroeder, "Conference Keynote Address," in *Consumer Protection in Postsecondary Education: Conference Report and Recommendations.* Denver, Colo.: Education Commission on the States, Report No. 53, June 1974.

34. Sandra L. Willett, "Consumer Protection in Higher Education," *Liberal Education,* May 1975, pp. 161-172.

35. Robert G. Peterson, "The College Catalog as a Contract," *Educational Record,* Vol. 51, Summer 1970, pp. 260-266.

36. Louis W. Bender, "Can Your Catalogue Stand the Test of FTC Guidelines?" *Phi Beta Kappan,* December 1975.

37. Elaine H. El-Khawas, "Consumerism Comes to Campus," *CASE Currents,* February 1976, pp. 4-6. See also her *New Expectations for Fair Practice: Suggestions for Institutional Review.* Washington, D.C.: American Council on Education, 1976.

38. Carnegie Council on Policy Studies in Higher Education, *Fair Practices in Higher Education.* San Francisco: Jossey-Bass, Inc., Publishers, 1979.

39. Stephen Joel Trachtenberg and Lawrence C. Levy, "In Search of Warm Bodies," *Change,* Summer 1973, pp. 51-57.

40. Edward B. Fiske, "Hard-Hit Schools Turn to Marketers," *New York Times,* January 22, 1977.

41. *Business Week,* "Colleges Learn the Hard Sell," February 14, 1977, pp. 92, 94; "Company Courses Go Collegiate," February 26, 1979, pp. 90, 92. Roger Ricklefs, "Changing Courses: Squeezed for Money, A Number of Colleges Revamp Curriculums," *Wall Street Journal,* February 18, 1975, pp. 1, 34. "Universal U.: New York New School Rides on Rising Wave of Adult Education," *Wall Street Journal,* January 13, 1978, p. 1.

42. John C. Sawhill, "Lifelong Learning: Scandal of the Next Decade?" *Change,* December-January 1978-79, pp. 7-8.

43. Lorenzo Middleton, "Student-Hungry Colleges Adopt New Techniques to Market Their Wares," *Chronicle of Higher Education,* April 30, 1979, pp. 3-4. Kotler, "Strate-

gies for Marketing." Edward B. Fiske, "The Marketing of the Colleges," *Atlantic Monthly*, October 1979, pp. 93-98.

44. Carnegie Council, *Fair Practices*, pp. 25-26.

45. "Extensive Critique of Extensions," April 2, 1978, Sec. 4, p. 6.

46. Robert Lindsey, "For Sale: Ph.D.'s, Etc.," *New York Times*, May 1, 1977. John Bear, *College Degrees by Mail: A Comprehensive Guide to Nontraditional Education*. Mendicino, Calif.: Rafton and Bear, 1978.

47. Ari L. Goldman, "Debating 'Life Experience,'" *New York Times*, February 4, 1979, Sec. 4, pp. 9, 18.

48. "Under Attack: College Credits for Living," April 16, 1979.

49. Jane Gribbin Andrews, "Off-Campus Education: Academic Colonialism," *Change*, February 1979, pp. 54-55. Andy Pasztor and Rich Jaroslovsky, "Question of Degree: Colleges Find Dollars in Branches for Adults, but Some Lose Quality," *Wall Street Journal*, May 21, 1979.

50. Andrews, "Off-Campus Education."

51. "Some Colleges are Bobbing Up Everywhere," January 7, 1979, p. 20.

52. Ibid.

53. Theodore Levitt, "Production-Line Approach to Service," *Harvard Business Review*, Vol. 50, September-October 1972, p. 41.

54. Sharon Johnson, "Subcontracted Courses Stir Controversy," *New York Times*, September 11, 1977, p. 15. Beverly T. Watkins, "Educational Brokers: Threat to Academic Standards?" *Chronicle of Higher Education*, June 20, 1977, p. 6.

55. Carnegie Council, *Fair Practices*, pp. 41-42.

56. "Many Career Schools Turn Education into a Fast Buck Industry" (First of 8-part "Spotlight" series on the profit-making vocational education industry), *Boston Globe*, March 25, 1974. Edward B. Fiske, "Schools for Profit" (3-part series), *New York Times*, July 25, 26, 27, 1979.

57. Carnegie Council, *Fair Practices*, pp. 43-44.

58. Ibid., pp. 34, 36, 38-39.

59. "Many Career Schools," *Boston Globe*. Fiske, "Marketing of Colleges."

60. Carnegie Council, *Fair Practices*.

61. "Many Career Schools," *Boston Globe*. Fiske, "Schools for Profit."

62. Middleton, "Student-Hungry Colleges."

63. Carnegie Council, *Fair Practices*, pp. 71-72.

64. Fiske, "Marketing of Colleges."

65. Fred Harvey Harrington, *The Future of Adult Education*. San Francisco: Jossey-Bass, Inc., Publishers, 1977.

66. David J. Graulich, "Graying of Campus: Adult Students Alter Face of U.S. Colleges as Enrollments Falter," *Wall Street Journal*, January 24, 1977, pp. 1, 20. Edith Brill Roth, "Education's Gray Boom," *American Education*, July 1978, pp. 6-11.

67. Walter Perry, *The Open University*, San Francisco: Jossey-Bass, Inc., Publishers, 1977. George W. Bonham, "The Open University: Lessons for the Future," *Change*, November 1978, pp. 14-15.

68. Paul L. Little and J. Richard Gilliland, "OASES in Oklahoma," *Library Journal*, July 1977, pp. 1458-1461.

69. Sawhill, "Lifelong Learning."

70. Karen Arenson, "Colleges Find that Adult Market Brings Risks as Well as Rewards," *New York Times*, September 9, 1979, Sec. 12, pp. 1, 12.

The Current Marketing Environment in Higher Education
by William Ihlanfeldt

Recent admonitions in the American Assembly's report on the *Integrity of Higher Education*[1] and in the Carnegie Council's report on *Fair Practices in Higher Education*[2] require a pause to reflect. Whether one agrees or demurs, at this forum a response is necessary either as a review of our own institutional practices, as a public reply, or both. To an extent these statements are to be applauded, since every industry must be reminded periodically of desired standards and acceptable levels of performance. Yet many of the practices referenced have been common occurrences in American higher education for the last two decades. The supposition underlying the belated nature of these reports is that the credibility of American higher education has been seriously undermined. The challenge has been succinctly stated by the American Assembly: "Public confidence in American higher education has been eroded in recent years. Consensus on what constitutes legitimate higher education has been reduced, and expectations of it — and claims for it — have not been fulfilled."[3]

As I have suggested, the attendant problems itemized are quite similar to, if not the same as, those that have always plagued the education industry. Possibly the issues are of greater significance today because the imminent recession in higher education will affect us all. No institution will go unscathed.

The relationship of the role of marketing in higher education to what has been identified by these two reports as either questionable or unethical practices presents an opportunity to clarify the functional aspects of marketing. Furthermore, I will argue that the adoption and implementation of a comprehensive marketing plan by management will permit colleges and universities to become more responsive to constituent needs.

However, the current marketing environment in higher education is, at best, a response to a series of problems facing one of this nation's largest service industries. I wish to emphasize the word *service* because, as much as any other factor, the desire to serve personal and vested interests at the expense of societal needs may be the root of the problems we face as managers of the industry. These problems include costs increasing faster than revenues, excess capacity brought about by poor planning and inadequate responses to consumer interest, low levels of user satisfaction resulting in high attrition, and our own inabilities to define and differentiate both the programs we offer and the audiences we intend to serve. I recall one monograph published in 1968 entitled *The College Environment*[4] that may have provided an early insight when it concluded there are more differences among students than among institutions.

Although the evolution of a market orientation may be a partial answer to these problems, the present marketing environment in higher education is more instructive and developmental than operational. One does not have to look beyond the advertisements in the *Chronicle of Higher Education* or to attend conferences sponsored by the Council for Advancement and Support of Education and the American Council on Education to recognize that the current state of the art of marketing in higher education is exploratory. With this fact in mind, I hope I will be able to add to our understanding of marketing as it applies to admissions and the student market. Eventually, I will concentrate on what we know about student markets and the relationship between price and market position, but I would like to begin by sharing a couple of experiences I had early in my professional career.

As a newcomer to the admissions business in the fall of 1960, I was invited, together with another member of the admissions staff, to the president's office of the small, private, two-year, women's college for which we were working. The president of this Midwestern college was 33 years of age and also new to his job. He had, within the year, assumed the responsibilities of a college that was having serious enrollment and financial problems. One of his first decisions was to replace the admissions staff. All members of the new staff were male, and three of the four were recent college graduates. We each were assigned a territory in the central part of the United States, which included as many as six states, and in my first year I traveled over 60,000 miles. I spent as much time in hotels as I did in secondary schools talking with college counselors, for there were few students who were interested in this college.

On this particular day in 1960, however, the president was not interested in discussing our present recruitment activities; instead, he had a new proposal in mind. He wanted to discuss the possibilities of developing a California market for this Midwestern college. He emphasized the rapidly expanding population of the state but failed to consider the burgeoning growth of higher education within the state, the diverse nature of the population, the percentage of high school graduates that attended college outside of the state, or the likelihood that a substantial investment would be required to develop name recognition. Rather, he thought that if two members of the admissions staff spent two weeks visiting secondary schools in Southern California with the carrot of full scholarships, counselors and prospective students would indeed be interested. It was assumed, moreover, that this was just a beginning. Once we got our foot in the door, good students would attract other good students who would be willing to pay their own way. During our two-week sojourn in Los Angeles, we visited almost 100 secondary schools, offered full scholarships at every stop, and failed to recruit one student.

As I reflected upon that experience, it became obvious that we were totally unprepared to make such a recruitment effort and that had we done some market research, either we would not have gone or our approach would have been entirely different. Clearly, we had little or no understanding of market behavior and particularly those factors that tend to influence college choice. Such research was in its embryonic stages, but of greater significance was that we apparently did not know how to proceed to make an informed decision. Today, although ad hominem market decisions are made on a regular basis by college and university administrators, market information is readily available. The administrators of any institution have access to data that can permit well-defined choices.

If such information had been readily available to us in 1960, we could have quickly determined that such a short-term investment venture was inappropriate without considerable market cultivation. Thanks to the work of Alexander Astin and others over the past 20 years, we now know that few students travel more than 500 miles to college; that those who do are either relatively affluent, black, or both; and that reputation, program, location, and costs are the primary quantifiable variables affecting college choice. On the basis of these factors, since there were many colleges in the state of California with a more attractive market position than the Midwestern college I represented, the goal of its president would have been frustrated, regardless of a substantial investment in market penetration.

Another experience I would like to share, and one that should serve to remind us that the current state of recruitment is not so different, was a typical admissions activity in the summer of 1960.

A group of us admissions representatives were gathered in the college counseling offices at Glenbrook High School, now Glenbrook North High School, in Northbrook, Illinois. We were perusing the resumes of hundreds of secondary school graduates who were still seeking admission to college. Gary Mills, the college counselor at Glenbrook, had developed a national college placement service, and if memory serves me right, the responsibility for this service was assumed by the National Association of College Admissions Counselors. Each day, during those summer months, as few as 5 and as many as 25 college representatives would review the dossiers of aspiring college students. Of course, most of the college representatives who visited the placement center contended that their enrollments were sound, but they were searching for just one more unusually "talented" student.

For most of the colleges that were visiting the center at Glenbrook High School in 1960, the situation has really never changed over the past 20 years. There has always been room for one more student. Just when the representatives of these schools thought they were entering a period of stable or increasing enrollments with demand slightly in excess of the number of spaces available, their presidents would decide to increase the size of the entering class, or another state college or community college would open its doors within their principal market area. For all except a few of the 2,400 four-year institutions, shortfalls in expected enrollments have been more the norm than the exception.

For almost every admissions representative employed by a struggling institution and on the college-night circuit, sales marketing has been the name of the game. Many of these representatives neither live near the institution they represent nor spend much time on their campuses, and it has not been an infrequent experience to find that an admissions officer represents more than one school. Until recently, there has been little or no discussion, either formally or informally, about the nature of institutional markets, the pattern of student decisions, the effectiveness of different communication methods, or the quality of the educational experience at various colleges and universities. Before the mid 1960s, market research was limited to overlap studies by Dean Whitla at Harvard, and attitudinal research was just beginning at the National Merit Scholarship Corporation under Astin and Nichols. *Who Goes Where to College?*[5] was a book still to be written, and the misuses of the university, later defined by Clark Kerr,[6] were well enshrined in practice.

As we look at the current admissions marketing environment, there are a few recruitment methods being employed that are of questionable value and are viewed by some educators with disdain. In response to annual shortfalls in enrollment in the 1970s, numerous institutions have adopted what I prefer to call maverick tactics in an effort to redress their enrollment problems. Some of these were cited by Edward Fiske in an article entitled "The Marketing of the Colleges."[7] These could be defined generically as follows:

• The use of premiums that include tuition discounts and financial coupons offered to currently enrolled students for each new student they attract.

• The offering of no-need scholarships with the idea that talented students attract other talented students.

• The negotiation of financial aid packages, a practice that has been quite common historically in recruiting athletes and virtuosos.

• The employment of unaffiliated head-hunters who use the title consultants.

• The installment of a contract franchise admissions operation in which an external agency assumes the responsibilities for meeting enrollment goals.

• The attempt through promotion to fudge reality in terms of the location of the college and the quality of the experience offered.

Enrollment successes attributed to such activities have been, at best, short-lived. In analyzing these practices I am reminded of one of Philip Kotler's marketing axioms — that the best way to kill a bad product is to advertise it.

One story that I would like to share involves the problem of fudging reality or stretching the truth. Admissions representatives have been well known for telling it the way they would like to see it rather than the way it is. A friend of mine who represented a rather small college adjacent to a rather small pond used to tell prospects that there was a lake on the campus and that sailing on the lake was a common activity. One September a new student arrived with a sailboat 30 feet long on a trailer attached to the family car. Since the alleged lake was no more than 150 feet long and 100 feet wide, one can imagine the embarrassment. This is just a single rather dramatic example of how the gap is created between expectations and ultimate perceptions that often contributes to problems of attrition.

In the more typical admissions operations, markets are neither targeted nor segmented, and the secondary school visit retains its position as the dominant method of personally contacting prospective students in the traditional college cohort. For the most part the student recruitment effort remains a shotgun approach represented by an added set of promotional activities that are appearing with greater frequency and acceptability. These would include the following:

- The use of both commercial and public service advertisements.
- The development of logos, catchy phrases, and testimonials that seek to increase name recognition.
- The more extensive involvement, on a systematic basis, of the use of faculty, alumni, and undergraduates as well as their parents.
- The use of the office of the president, including direct contact with prospective students and their families.
- The use of consultants, many of whom have a background in development rather than admissions, with the intent of upgrading the quality of the promotional efforts and the efficiency of the office.

However, if there is anything new about the universal management of college admissions, it is the large scale use of direct mail and the participation in a phenomenon known as the college fair. The increased use of direct mail to virgin populations was stimulated by the creation of the Student Search Service, a program which has been offered by the College Board since 1972 and permits colleges to directly contact prospective students currently enrolled in secondary schools. As a result, some institutions have gone so far as to forfeit virtually all other recruitment efforts and now purchase the names of more than 75,000 prospective students annually. Because of this service and similar services offered by the American College Testing Program and other agencies, it is not uncommon for a high school senior to receive well over 100 pieces of unsolicited mail from as many different colleges. With the early access to thousands of names of secondary school students, colleges and universities have substantially intensified their promotional activities. One result has been an increase in the degree of "trade puffing"; a concept that is looked upon as a questionable practice by many persons involved in higher education, although it is sanctioned by the Federal Trade Commission.[8]

College fairs, which are sponsored by the National Association of College Admissions Counselors, bring together many colleges under the same roof to interact with prospective students in urban centers across the nation. To some colleges and many consumers the college fair is perceived as a vast supermarket with a zoo-like atmosphere; to other institutions with limited name recognition, it provides public exposure and some personal interaction with potential consumers.

Beyond these three efforts—the high school contact, increased uses of direct mail, and college fairs—the remaining time of admissions staffs is devoted to campus-based informational programs, interviews, phone contacts, application reviews, and conferencing with secondary school counselors. The problem with any or all of these activities is that there is little understanding as to their effectiveness. Yet, ironically, these promotional efforts, with limited evaluation, are replicated annually. The communication process between colleges and prospective students remains highly undifferentiated. However, as the press for students accelerates because of either real or anticipated excess capacity, increasing numbers of admissions directors, and in some instances even college presidents, are beginning to ask: Is there not a better way to achieve enrollment goals and moreover to improve the image of the institution?

With the advent of such questions, the use of the term *marketing* has become quite common, eulogized by some and abhorred by others. To those who find it ignoble, it is often translated to mean hard advertising, selling, or hucksterism. One does not have to look beyond the advertisements in Sunday newspapers to understand why. To those who recognize the merits of marketing in its simplest form, it is considered as a series of exchange relationships that satisfy genuine needs. Philip Kotler provides a more comprehensive definition: "Marketing is the analysis, planning, implementation, and control of carefully formulated programs designed to bring about voluntary exchanges of values with target markets for the purpose of achieving organizational objectives. It relys heavily on designing the organization's offering in terms of the target market's needs and desires, and on using effective pricing, communication, and distribution to inform, motivate and service the markets."[9]

Explicit in this definition is the focus on product design, pricing, communication, and distribution. This is referred to as the *marketing mix*, and many colleges and universities are in the process of tampering with one or more of these components. Unfortunately, many changes are made without any empirical bases. Rather, new efforts in one of these areas are undertaken because of market rumors or decisions made by the competition, or in the final analysis as a result of desperation.

Why Marketing?

The present focus on marketing in higher education is, indeed, a response to real or anticipated problems of shortfalls in revenue and enrollment. Of course, institutions are affected differently. To many faculty and administrators the idea of marketing simply implies an expansion of promotional activities; to others it is the application of a new language to the same old recruitment efforts; but to a few, whose numbers are growing, it is a methodology that will provide for an improved educational experience, much more oriented to the needs and interests of the consumer and of society.

The methods of selling higher education over the past 30 years have followed a similar reformation that transpired earlier in the profit sector. First, there was a production-promotion response to the market — a "take it or leave it" phase, which existed as long as the demand exceeded the supply of what was considered a desirable good. Second, the emphasis shifted to sales. This phase exists in an environment where there is an adequate number of consumer options available, but the competition exists for the so-called right student for the right school. This approach might best be defined as a sorting process, resulting in a state of equilibrium. In the third phase, supply exceeds demand, and the competition for consumer interests forces a reevaluation of the current services provided. Today, within many institutions, programs are being reevaluated in relation to potential markets. Consequently, there is greater management interest in *market research* and *consumer satisfaction*. Such an organizational response signifies the emergence of a marketing-oriented institution.

Marketing, in its fullest sense, would involve the entire institution in a coordinated and integrated effort to reevaluate programs, study student demography, and assess the relationship of the two in terms of market interests. With few exceptions, however, marketing as currently practiced in higher education has emphasized seduction through communication, and the sales approach remains dominant. Because the emphasis has been on "process" rather than "product," much of the interest in marketing has been admissions but not institutionally oriented. However, I do not intend to imply that by adopting an institutional marketing orientation, capricious consumer interests should take precedence over academic concerns. Rather, I expect that as educational institutions seek to accommodate more fully the needs of current students, the result of a more satisfying experience will be greater economic stability, if not greater demand for higher education.

The era we are about to enter requires new responses from all institutions but especially from the substantial number of colleges and universities that have always had rather weak market positions. The demographics are stacked against most institutions, and although I do not intend to reiterate the market trends that appear with considerable frequency in the most pedestrian of publications, I would like to emphasize the nature of the problem by interpreting a few trends and, possibly, by offering a different perspective.

▪ If the institutional objective is to maintain current enrollments among the traditional population (18-24 years old), then the college or university must attract an increasing share of a decreasing market. This goal is not likely to be realized at the vast majority of institutions.

▪ If a college or university is able to maintain its present enrollment, it will most likely be achieved at the expense of quality. The academic quality of all student bodies will decline.

▪ Migration patterns of students, and particularly of families to Southern states, will compound institutional enrollment problems in the Northern industrial states. Because of this family migration, current forecasts of the decline in Northern states are understated.

▪ The percentage of students enrolled part-time and in nondegree programs will increase, and the numbers enrolled will vary inversely with employment, particularly in the community colleges. As a result, participation rates will be adversely affected, particularly in transfer programs.

▪ The problem of declining enrollments will not be solved simply by recruiting nontraditional students. Few institutions have assessed, and few will be able to afford, the extra costs of educating nontraditional students.

▪ The enrollments in proprietary institutions will continue to increase unless some parts of higher education become less traditional in their practices — e.g., location, scheduling, and vocational orientation — and more aggressive in their pricing policies in order to produce the revenue required to meet the educational needs of the adult learner.

▪ Of the traditional cohort, there will be four types of students, not necessarily mutually exclusive, who will be interested in higher education: those who are genuinely interested in learning; those with extracurricular interests that can only be pursued by enrolling in college; those for whom higher education is a family tradition; and those whose career goals require a specific curriculum experience.

- If higher education is to have a renewed credibility, many programs will have to be packaged differently, and the product should not be cheapened through such practices as (1) early admission to college before completion of secondary school, (2) acceptance of unqualified students to accelerated and combined degree programs, and (3) the awarding of substantial amounts of credit through examination and for life's experiences.

This changing market milieu will stimulate the development of a new educational environment. Some colleges and universities will be able to respond adeptly, but others because of limited resources and poor management will respond with errant decisions. In such an environment, ethics will be rightly questioned. In the area of college admissions, however, inquiry about ethical behavior has had a certain permanence, partly because there has always been a substantial number of struggling colleges where survival has been the dominant theme, but mainly because admissions personnel, although often knowledgeable spectators on their own campuses, have not been participants in the decision process. They seldom have been asked whether the implementation of a new program was a good idea, but they have always been expected to promote it. This approach creates a production-promotion mentality similar to that of an automobile salesman. He may not like the automobile he has to sell, but no one asks him about market interest or automobile design. Nevertheless, if he wants to eat, he must sell the product.

A New Opportunity

The period of uncertainty ahead will provide directors of admissions with a new opportunity to play a significant role in the direction of their institutions. If they continue to perceive their role as recruiters, selling a product in which they may or may not believe, then they will remain outsiders, operating on the boundaries of institutions. On the other hand, if they view their role as a source of market and consumer information and can successfully communicate such information internally, they will redefine their position as directors of marketing, catalysts for change.

To redefine this role, they must involve others not only as sources of information but as participants in the communication process. As a director of marketing, the director of admissions should perceive the role as orchestrating a communication process involving, on the one hand, the faculty, staff, undergraduates, and alumni of the institution and, on the other, prospective students, parents, friends, and secondary school personnel. Ultimately this communications network should include opinion leaders at the local, state, and national levels capable of influencing not only prospective students but prospective donors and public officials as well. The support of all these groups is vital to the success of the institution. This network must be systematically created and managed, but it cannot be any better than the quality of the information gathered and transmitted.

Every institution, whether it serves primarily a local, a regional, or a national clientele, should be able to identify its primary and secondary markets, as well as its market position among its principal competitors. Although there now exists ample research on the college experience and on student market behavior, such information is still rarely utilized in institutional or admissions planning. To emphasize the significance of research in marketing and to assist in the translation of what is known, I would like to restate some of the findings[10] and then present a planning matrix to interpret or to affect market behavior.

- Forty percent of all first-time college students apply to only the college they intend to enter, and 18 percent apply to only two institutions. Thus, approximately 58 percent apply to no more than two institutions.

- More successful students are more likely to apply and enroll in private institutions, assuming financial resources are available.

- In contrast to the prevailing opinion that students are extremely mobile, in excess of 90 percent of all first-time college students attend an institution within 500 miles of their homes. Moreover, students tend to enroll in their first-choice college when it is near their homes.

- The degree of mobility appears to be influenced to a great extent by the socioeconomic background of the family, and the number of colleges located within a particular region of the country.

- Students living in the East and the Midwest tend to enroll in colleges closer to home because of not only the number but also the perceived quality of the colleges in these areas.

- Students in the West either travel very few miles or considerable distances. Apparently, this is a reflection of the community college system within the state of California as well as the market position of Eastern schools.
- However, regardless of region, students from more affluent backgrounds, exclusive of blacks, are more mobile with regard to college choice.
- Black students are relatively mobile for three reasons: the concentration of black colleges in the South, the extensive recruitment practices of predominantly Northern white institutions, and the current emphasis upon education as a means of socioeconomic advancement.
- Regardless of financial aid resources, students from lower-class homes, and particularly those who are Catholic, are the least mobile.
- No more than 25 percent of the families whose children take the SATs can afford the average full price of a public institution, and no more than 16 percent can meet the average full expense of a typical private institution.
- The timing of the announcement of financial aid is critical in determining the choice of college. The earlier such information is available, the more likely a student with limited resources will consider private institutions and major state institutions. The longer such information is delayed, the more likely it is that not only college choice may be limited but that access may be denied.

As I stated earlier, when students are asked why they considered a given set of colleges, the following criteria are dominant: program, reputation, price, and location. Whether a student will focus regionally or nationally in selecting a set of colleges according to the aforementioned criteria depends, to a great extent, upon his or her psychological mobility. However, of those colleges that meet the criteria and are considered as final choices, the one in which a candidate is most likely to enroll is determined by noncognitive factors. These would include the secondary school attended, the education of the parents, the family's socioeconomic status, the experiences of older siblings, extracurricular interests, and religious preference.

The above information is useful in determining a college's primary and secondary markets, but with regard to the issue of geographical mobility, the dominant factors will be a student's prior academic performance and the family's financial strength. A market interpretation of the interaction between student ability and family finances is necessary for a more complete understanding of the college decision-making process, and to suggest a method by which admissions staffs can evaluate their markets and projected yields. A yield may be defined in various ways: as the response rate to a general or a restricted mailing to a pool of prospects; as the percent of those students enrolling who were initially contacted through some mailing or other forms of communication; or as the percent of students enrolling who were admitted to the institution. To assist in visualizing the influences of student ability and family finances on mobility, I would like to present a matrix (see Figure 1) that can be referred to as the Student Mobility Paradigm.[11] This analysis is pursued with the hope that as we look to the future such information will improve admissions planning and reduce the tendency to adopt capricious recruitment practices.

Clearly, in terms of college choice, a student with considerable ability and with no financial need is more geographically mobile than another student with limited ability and high financial need. Although such a hypothesis could be justified on the basis of common sense, the paradigm presented is an attempt to depict graphically the degree of student mobility within market segments that can be determined by empirical research. Ability in this instance is arbitrarily subdivided along a continuum 1 through 4, with 4 representing the highest quartile. Ability could be defined as performance on a standardized test, grades received in secondary school, or a combination of both factors. Financial need is also defined along a continuum that includes high, moderate, low, and no need. Those prospects who fall in the no-need category may or may not have applied for financial assistance.

One assumption that can be made, based upon empirical evidence, is that students who fall into cell H1 (high need, low ability) are the least mobile geographically, and students who fall in cell N4 (no need, high ability) are the most mobile. In fact, students who fall in the H1 cell are also the least likely to attend college immediately after secondary school. If they do pursue a postsecondary education experience, it is likely to be either at a community college or at a proprietary school, assuming that one or the other is located in proximity to their homes. Generally, this statement would apply to all those students who fall within cells located in the first quadrant, which includes cells H1, H2, M1, and M2. However, because of the relative nature of a continuum, the behavior is more predictable in

Figure 1. Student Mobility Paradigm

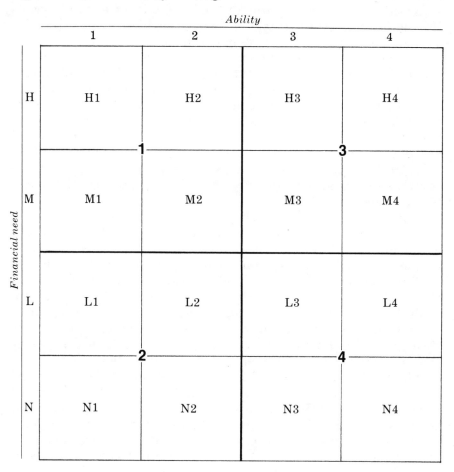

H1 than in any of the other three cells of quadrant 1. In contrast, students who fall in all the cells in quadrant 4, which include cells L3, L4, N3, and N4, are quite mobile. Students who fall in the N4 cell are the most mobile, and in fact they apply to more than four colleges and are accepted by almost as many. As one moves along a continuum from H1 to H4, the likelihood of a student attending college increases considerably. The same conclusion can be applied to those students who fall along a continuum from H1 to N1. Students who fall along the continuum H4 to N4 will be increasingly more mobile geographically with regard to college choice. One could come to a similar conclusion with regard to students in the cells along the continuum N1 through N4, but students who fall in cells N1 and N2 will not have as many choices available to them; thus, they are not likely to apply to as many colleges.

Summarily, this paradigm suggests that participation rates are primarily a function of ability and family wealth. To a great extent, participation rates at the lower end of the continuum have been inflated by the infusion of government student assistance, but these funds do not compensate for ability or for interest in education. An institution that attracts a high percentage of students who would be categorized as falling within the cells in quadrant 1 and 2 should expect a high attrition rate. Moreover, the participation of these students in higher education will be inversely proportional to employment opportunities.

As implied previously, black students who would fall in cell H4 appear to be far more mobile than students from other races and ethnic groups. Although students who fall within cell N4 are quite mobile geographically, students from Hispanic backgrounds, excluding Cuban nationals, would be the least mobile within that cell because of characteristics related to family history. These would include less assimilation, language barriers, Catholic background, less internal and external pressures to seek socioeconomic mobility through education. Succinctly, the available evidence suggests that a student with considerable ability is likely to select a college within commuter distance if his family ties are quite strong and his parents have no more than a high school education and limited financial resources. Despite financial aid, the interaction effects of parents' education, family ties, and limited income impose psychological restrictions in terms of college choice and student mobility.

The Student Mobility Paradigm, in addition to permitting a segmented market analysis of behavior with regard to college choice, also can be used to assess the educational needs of prospective students within a given market area and to determine whether those needs are being met by the educational institutions within that region. In other words, an admissions staff should evaluate the potential of a given geographic market in terms of the number of students who might fall within the various cells and how that distribution compares with students who are currently attending college within that region. This matching process also provides some guidance with regard to the amount of resources required to attract and to serve students in a given market area who fall within any one of the cells. For example, a college that would tend to attract a significant number of students who fell within the first quadrant should be prepared to provide a variety of academic support services. In contrast, the same kinds of services would not be required for a college that was able to attract students from either quadrant 3 or quadrant 4. Of course, a college attracting more students from within quadrant 1 or quadrant 3 must bear the greater cost of financial aid compared to a college attracting more students from quadrant 2 and quadrant 4. Thus, one must ask: How much diversity can any one college afford? This question should be asked in terms of providing not only financial assistance but also necessary support services.

Market Position and Price

As the tuition gap between the public and private sectors continues to increase, one alternative adopted by many private colleges has been to engage in practices of price discounting, independent of financial needs, as a market incentive, and as a process to permit students to make an educational rather than a financial choice. The obvious question is, to what extent will these practices affect college choice? The answer depends upon the degree of interest a student has in a given college, the extent of the student's willingness for self-help, and the price variation among a set of colleges in which he or she is interested.

Again, I would like to turn to the Student Mobility Paradigm to explore further the relation between price and market position. Students in cells M3 and M4 are defined, for purposes here, as those who might be able to attend public institutions without any financial assistance, but who would need considerable aid to attend an independent institution. The question then becomes whether the independent institution can neutralize the price differences by offering an attractive financial aid package or whether a student is sufficiently interested in the private institution to want to invest substantially in his or her education through self-help. Thus, the stronger the market position of an independent college, the more self-help it can expect from its financial aid candidates. Conversely, a private college with limited visibility might improve its market position by limiting the degree of expected self-help and increasing the amount of grant assistance within the context of financial need. However, if the student's first-choice college is a public institution, it is probable that no degree of price discounting will change the candidate's mind.

As indicated, the degree to which self-help can be required is related to the market position of the college. Those few colleges that have extremely strong national market positions can expect a specified amount of self-help from every candidate who applies and qualifies for financial assistance. These colleges do not have to vary the self-help component in relation to the total financial need. The weaker the market position in relation to a college's primary competition, the more likely it is that such a college will have to reduce the amount of self-help required. Therefore, the market position of a college would affect the financial aid packaging policies for all students who fell within cells M3, M4, L3, and L4.

For all types of high-priced institutions, however, students falling in cells L3 and L4 appear to be the most difficult to attract.[12] Students within these cells come from families who would be expected to contribute $4,000 to $6,000 a year to their education. They are able to attend a public university within their state for approximately $3,400. Therefore, even though these students would receive some financial assistance at many private and out-of-state public institutions, meeting the remaining costs of attendance would require families to sacrifice more than meeting the total costs of attendance at a public university within the state. Such families also may be looking toward the future when they will have other children entering college. For these families it is a matter of *marginal utility:* Is the perceived quality of the benefits to be received as great or greater than the price differences between the two colleges being considered? The marketing technique applied by some independent colleges in an effort to attract students within cells L3 and L4 is to eliminate self-help entirely and to offer grant assistance in excess of a student's financial need. The amount of the discount required is directly related to the degree of interest in the institution and the extent to which a family believes its financial needs have been met.

If an institution wishes to improve its market position, the creation of a special program may have the same effect as the offering of more attractive financial aid packages. In fact, special programs within an institution may have a market position separate from that of the institution. One example is an honors program in medical education that admits the student to medical school as an entering freshman. Another example is offering combined B.A. and M.A. degrees within the period normally required for a bachelor's degree alone. These kinds of programs are not only a form of portfolio packaging, they are also a form of price discounting. If a student is able to accelerate his or her education and thus save a year of tuition and foregone income, then this is a very attractive financial aid package even if a student does not have a financial need. However, at the same time, these types of program options can result in shoddy or unethical market incentives if offered to unqualified prospective students. There is only a limited number of colleges and universities prepared to offer such programs, and there is only a small percentage of students who are eligible.

A Market-Sensitive Financial Aid Program

Under a market-sensitive model, the amount of self-help required in relation to grant assistance would vary, within reason, across groups of candidates and/or from individual candidate to individual candidate within groups. The variation in self-help would be based upon the following: the market position of a college as compared to other colleges in which the candidate is interested; the relative market position of a program or a school within a university compared to the relative market position of other programs or schools within the same university and of the institution as a whole; the market position of a college in relation to student ability and financial need as defined by the Student Mobility Paradigm; and the market position of a candidate as compared to the market position of an institution. As a matter of clarification each of these concepts will be expanded.

1. The market position of a college as compared to other colleges in which the candidate is interested — each financial aid form identifies the other colleges to which a prospective student is likely to apply. This information permits an institution to assess its relative market position.

2. The relative strength of the market position of a program or a school within an institution — one or both may have a stronger market position than the institution. For example, within a region, a program in fine arts may have a very strong market position compared to similar programs offered by other institutions. A program's demand is determined by the number of applicants over time compared to other programs offered by the institution. In this instance, students accepted to a program in great demand may be offered more loan and work assistance and less grant assistance. Another example would be accelerated programs whereby a stu-

dent completes both a bachelor's and master's degree within a four-year time frame. Since such a program already provides for a reduction in the required investment in education, it should be possible to offer less grant assistance and more self-help within the context of financial need. Conversely, a candidate with strong credentials who applies to a program with a weak market position would be offered more grant assistance and less self-help.

3. The market position of a college in relation to student ability and financial need as defined by the Student Mobility Paradigm — since students in cells H3 and H4 are not very mobile with regard to college choice, the greater the amount of self-help, the less likely students in these cells will attend a given college, if another located nearer a student's home offers less self-help and more grant assistance. The idea of absorbing considerable debt to acquire an education is a concept foreign to students from such families. Thus, for students who fall in these cells, the greater the distance between a student's residence and the college, the less responsive a student will be to a large self-help component. In this instance this analysis would apply to any college irrespective of the strength of the market position. Those colleges that apply a policy of a set amount of self-help for all financial aid candidates may want to reconsider their positions with regard to students from such backgrounds. The same analysis can be applied to students within cells M3 and M4, but to a lesser extent. The prospects that fall in these two cells will be influenced by the amount of self-help required by a private school, particularly if the parents of these students have graduated from a public university and if these students also are considering a public institution with a good market position.

4. Finally, the credentials of a candidate as compared to the market position of a college or university — is the candidate's market position stronger than the institution's as compared to the typical student who enrolls? Within the context of financial need, it may be desirable to offer these students substantial grant assistance in relation to self-help.

The awarding of financial assistance based upon this model can be effective in attracting those students who are undecided with regard to college choice. At the margin, the adoption of the concept of competitive financial aid packaging is an effective method of improving a college's market position. Such a process is really no different than the type of price discounting that takes place in other industries and has proven to be a successful marketing technique.

However, the evidence does suggest that, in the aggregate, students with financial need will elect to attend their first-choice college regardless of how financial aid is packaged as long as their families believe their financial need has been met.

Commentary

The credibility of higher education has rightfully been questioned by the American Assembly and the Carnegie Council. From my perspective, higher education has come to mean too many different things to too many people without a common standard of acceptable intellectual performance. Over the past decade the interests of many institutions and many individuals have concentrated more upon credentialing and less upon academic substance. One result has been for the public to perceive the higher education experience as something one digests quickly as a means to an end. Not only academic institutions but also national service organizations have proliferated programs with the intent to increase demand and revenues without addressing questions related to educational outcomes. The emphasis has been on promotion and sales. The implicit consumer message, therefore, ought to have been caveat emptor. Too many unfulfilled promises have resulted in high attrition rates that have often been rationalized euphemistically as the "stop-out" problem. Moreover, the system has been perpetuated and enrollments artificially inflated through the largess of excessive government student assistance with minimum quality controls governing the equity of these programs. In some areas the best that can be said about government student aid is that it has deferred entry into the labor market of students who have little interest in education and who had no other options.

As I wrote this paper, I could not help but feel that the analysis of the current marketing environment in higher education was like attempting to fill a void. A void in the sense that for the most part the "hyped" promotional activities currently presented on behalf of colleges and universities represent only one component of marketing as defined by the academic theorists. The problem is that many institutions, in response to revenue needs and often encouraged by their national associations, either have attempted to attract new markets — such as nontraditional and foreign students — without the capability to accommodate such students or have created new programs to attract new markets without any systematic effort to assess market interests. The missing components in the marketing equation have been the lack of institutional analysis and market research. Notwithstanding the available market information derived by independent investigators, the managers of most colleges and universities have been unable to translate such data to the circumstances of their own institutions. Moreover, because of the highly transient nature of personnel in the admissions profession and because of their historic place in the organizational structure, market information that crosses their desks often is not related to their own problems and seldom transcends the boundaries of their departments.

The past and present role of marketing in higher education remains highly sales oriented. Generally, admissions representatives have been expected to sell more of the same with the expectation that like Geritol with plenty of rest and exercise, the experience will make one feel better. However, as the consumer becomes increasingly informed and legally protected, and as the market shifts from an ambiance of caveat emptor to one of caveat venditor, the future emphasis on marketing in higher education is more likely to be upon product development than the continued enhancement of the promotional process. Historically, the demand for higher education has been eternally stimulated; however, if excess capacity is to be minimized in this new decade, demand must be stimulated by internal factors, namely the quality of the experience. This is not to gainsay there are numerous colleges and universities that insist upon quality and serve their constituencies well. Unfortunately, they serve a minority of students, and therefore society's needs are not being fulfilled. The idea of lifelong learning exists because of the motivation of a few and is yet to be understood by the many. As long as higher education is interpreted to mean a better job and more money and continues to be sold on that basis, the future of many colleges and universities may be in doubt.

I have inserted into this discussion a method of analyzing market behavior through a matrix referred to as the Student Mobility Paradigm. The intent is to encourage admissions officers, as well as other administrators, to become far more systematic in assessing their markets as well as their institution's position within a market hierarchy. The development of such an understanding among administrators would enhance the likelihood that they would have more control over the destiny of their institutions. A failure to grasp such information or to be uninterested will assure the continuation and possible expansion of charlatan-like practices that result in the unproductive use of scarce resources and further diminish the credibility of the industry.

References

1. American Assembly, *The Integrity of Higher Education*. Englewood Cliffs, N.J.: Prentice-Hall, Inc., 1979.
2. Carnegie Council on Policy Studies in Higher Education, *Fair Practices in Higher Education*. San Francisco: Jossey-Bass, Inc., Publishers, 1979.
3. American Assembly, *Integrity*, p. 4.
4. Alexander Astin, *The College Environment*. Washington, D.C.: American Council on Education, 1968.
5. Alexander Astin, *Who Goes Where to College?* Chicago: Science Research Association, 1965.
6. Clark Kerr, *The Uses of the University*. Cambridge, Mass.: Harvard University Press, 1963.
7. *Atlantic Monthly*, October 1979, pp. 93-98.
8. D. H. Sandage and R. V. Fryburger, *Advertising Theory and Practice*, 9th Edition. Homewood, Ill.: R. C. Irwin Incorporated, 1975.
9. Philip Kotler, *Marketing for Nonprofit Organizations*. Englewood Cliffs, N.J.: Prentice Hall, Inc., 1975, p. 5.
10. My statements are based upon the following reports: Alexander W. Astin, Margo R. King, and Gerald T. Richardson, *The American Freshman: National Norms for Fall 1965-1978*. Los Angeles: Laboratory for Research in Higher Education, Graduate School of Education, University of California; Cooperative Institutional Research Program, American Council on Education, 1965-1978. College Entrance Examination Board, *National Report, College Bound Seniors, 1978*. New York: College Entrance Examination Board, 1978. Thomas M. Corwin and Laura Kent, editors, *Tuition and Student Aid: Their Relation to College Enrollment Decisions*. Washington, D.C.: Policy Analysis Service, American Council on Education, May 1978. D. E. Lavin, *The Prediction of Academic Performance: A Theoretical Analysis and Review of Research*. New York: Department of Sociology, University of Pennsylvania; Russell Sage Foundation, 1965. Larry L. Leslie and Jonathan D. Fife, "The College Student Grant Study: The Enrollment and Attendance Impacts of Student Grant and Scholarship Programs," *Journal of Higher Education*, Vol. XLV, No. 9, December 1974, pp. 651-671. Richard Spies, *The Effect of Rising Costs on College Choice*. New York: College Entrance Examination Board, 1978. Michael L. Tierney, "The Impact of Financial Aid on Student Demand for Public/Private Higher Education." University Park, Pa.: Center for the Study of Higher Education, Pennsylvania State University, December 1978.
11. Concepts related to the Student Mobility Paradigm and market segmentation are presented in greater detail in my book *Achieving Optimal Enrollments and Tuition Revenues*. San Francisco: Jossey-Bass, Inc., Publishers, 1980.
12. Ted Bracken, *Enrolling the Class of 1978: An Analysis of the 1974 Student Market at Twenty-Three Private Institutions*. Hanover, N.H.: Consortium on Financing Higher Education, October 1975. Spies, *Rising Costs*.

Marketing Perspectives and Institutional Admissions Office Pressures for Meeting Enrollments

by John C. Hoy

Introduction

For its last meeting of the 1970s the American Council on Education chose the theme "Competition and Quality." The Annual ACE Forum, while not an occasion for sensing the cutting edge of higher education reform, does provide a sense of what is on the minds of policy makers and institutional leaders from across the nation. For most, it is principally an occasion to touch base with the perceptions and concerns of one's peers. The program is aimed at providing for discussion of trends that are already on top of the institution or will soon arrive on the doorstep. "Competition and Marketing" would have been a more appropriate title, for concern with issues of quality appeared to be a distinct afterthought in the minds of most attendees.

In session after session the terms *marketing, market forces, market share, market research, world markets, market penetration* resounded like words from a fresh vocabulary, a call to action and renewal. To watch the inflation-weary expressions of the presidents and deans of the nation's campuses ponder this significance was an experience entirely without parallel. The new vocabulary, while listened to with considerable interest, did not appear to gain much ground. Ears did perk up and then relax again as the term *strategic planning* came into play. There appeared to be an uneasy sense that these leaders had gathered to learn of new ways for bringing a modicum of order to the impending chaos of enrollment decline. The advocates of marketing and strategic planning were appropriately guarded in making promises but missionary in their dedication to describing this "new" means for survival.

How odd that higher education, so recently buffeted by the terms that students used to define the academy's cooptation by the military-industrial complex, should be engaged in listening so earnestly to the preemptive vocabulary of the advanced theories of the military and business establishments. I took it as no small compliment to our general intelligence that most participants walked away from these sessions skeptical, if not quite convinced that there had to be a better approach—one less dependent upon processes that have so little apparent kinship with the central modes of learning and open inquiry most reflective of the academic community. It was difficult for those assembled to embrace systems of action so alien to the processes of scholarship as to be beyond emulation: systems dedicated to selling a product sufficient to assure a profit or to render oneself invulnerable and one's opponent as potentially conquerable. The basic difference and the compelling argument against emulation seemed to focus on the use of such language itself.

The methods of academic life and its administration in pursuit of encouraging the intellectual community – a marketplace for ideas (if you will) – must of necessity be open and revealing of the sources of truth, wherever they may be found. When an approach to problem resolution is rife with jargon, is regularized and kept confidential or viewed as defensively strategic, the flow of ideas is, as a consequence, limited if not distorted. There appeared to be a disquieted sense of willingness to examine the question of applicability of techniques but no inclination to embrace what might prove to be antithetical to institutional integrity. No chord of antiphony was struck: resonance, yes, but resolution, no. The assembled educators talked of little other than the state of impending decline, but seemed disinclined to believe there were easy answers or ready techniques close at hand to mollify its impact. Yet, the vocabulary of marketing had taken another step forward in the language of higher education.

There are many of us who find disquieting the adaptation of terms and concepts inherent to business. We see their use by the academic community as a mixed blessing – more reflective of our own confusion and loss of direction than an indication of new departures. But it seems fruitless at this point, as the terms find a home on more and more campuses and in national academic assemblies as well as in the work of scholars and academic critics, to combat this expanding trend. Whatever our discomfort with notions and words borrowed from the corporate marketplace, the commitment to marketing in higher education is spreading and seems irreversible – what then does it imply?

As with most trends in higher education, the fruits of marketing are as mixed as the pressures that lead to their employment. Certainly when it is understood as a student-centered approach, marketing cannot be faulted as an honest tool intended for the use of consumer-responsive management. But the rush to the marketing banner by educators has resulted in a confusion of perspective and interpretations that cause skepticism and anguish in responsible educators. Critics of marketing in higher education see a danger of linking decision making exclusively to that which is materially profitable. Indeed, many advocates of the marketing system unabashedly recommend the abolition of programs and courses that are uneconomical and the creation or expansion of programs that pay.

Lyman A. Glenny lists this method of economizing among his collection of "old wives' tales and myths." Glenny's myth is stated as "all low-productivity degree programs should be eliminated." Rather, he suggests decisions on abolishing programs or courses should be based on complex factors. There are programs low in productivity and high in cost that are nonetheless essential for the good of society and the survival of culture and science. Therefore, such inquiry remains a primary responsibility of the university to sustain.[1]

Transferring marketing concepts from the marketplace to the campus can do irreparable disservice to the teaching-learning process. In the marketplace, losing money is a thing to be avoided. In education, losing a student can be an appropriate eventuality, even though every matriculated student brings to the private college an "unrestricted gift" of about $10,000 over four years.[2] Both in material and human terms a student enrolled is a precious gift.

Loss of the Individual

Considerations of human uniqueness and individual promise have become educationally archaic in recent years. Discussing the irreplaceable and irretrievable uniqueness of the individual student, the peculiar and specific worthiness of a young person with a mind in need of exposure, challenge, and cultivation, echoes some distant era focused on irrelevant cultivation of personal growth and nonutilitarian concerns with human development. Colleges and universities, as is true of other communities, have become preoccupied with issues of self-preservation and self-interest. The marketing of higher education may lead to the further distancing of institutions from the aspirations of individuals. There will be a tendency to view the public in increasingly well-defined aggregates of attitudinal, socioeconomic, and mobile age cohorts in various stages of responsiveness to the clues and cues provided them by institutions casting a wider and wider net — a net whose mesh is designed to at least delay (perhaps detain) a significant proportion of individuals in order to provide a catch sufficiently large enough to create a market. The individual seems less special as the pressure for enrollment maintenance heightens and the casting for participants broadens.

Yet the key for us as we consider marketing concepts is to avoid techniques and decisions based primarily on institutional self-interest. Our first consideration must be simply the good of those being served. We are helped toward this goal by sifting through the definitions of marketing that bombard us from so many quarters. A widely quoted and accepted definition comes from Philip Kotler who describes marketing as "the effective management by an organization of its exchange relations with its various markets and publics." He explains:

"All organizations depend upon exchange relations to attract resources that they need to convert them into useful products and services, and to distribute them efficiently to target markets. Marketing is a systematic approach to planning and achieving desired exchange relations with other groups. Marketing is concerned with developing, maintaining, and/or regulating exchange relations involving products, services, organizations, persons, places, or causes."[3]

Those of us who view with alarm the idea of promoting and selling higher education a la Madison Avenue take some comfort from the views of Kotler and even more perhaps from those of Peter Druckner who says that "marketing's purpose is to make selling superfluous."[4] It is clear, however, that many higher education administrators are listening to other voices, for gimmickry and the hard sell are being advanced every day by people in education posing as marketing experts. National meetings abound with such presentations, and the advertising revenue gathered by the *Chronicle of Higher Education* alone from the promotion of marketing is impressive. Marketing is "in"; management by objectives is "out"; and strategic planning is "around the corner."

When we view the tuition paid by an enrolled student as an unrestricted gift, we understand more clearly the desire of so many educational administrators to have their institutions grow a bit each year, just as we understand better the increasing pressures being exerted on admissions offices and officers across the land.

As the American academy prepares itself to enter this marketplace in earnest in the 1980s in order to sell its wares to a diminishing supply of its traditional customers, I would like to suggest it is still possible to pause for a moment to determine what such efforts will provide the exhibitor in both the near and longer term.

Let us make no mistake about it, higher education is about to witness the death of many salesmen, the mounting insolvency of a fair share of its competition, and the ruin of a significant portion of those institutions found increasingly in a position of not being able to satisfy just claims made upon them. We are familiar with the impact of failed corporations, and we are becoming aware of the tragedy associated with the failure of colleges.

One of the weaknesses that decades of unparalleled growth has fostered in the American academy has been its increasing reluctance and limited capacity to exhibit itself honestly. As higher education has become commonplace, so too has the rhetoric of intellectual endeavor. The revelation of the results of genuine intellectual inquiry and research has been popularized and sold cheaply to a public eager for good news. Higher education has reduced itself to the information demands of a media-hyped society.

Accepting growth as a way of life, higher education has become accustomed to *not* presenting itself for open inspection. Enveloped in processes of peer review and certification by professional guilds, colleges and universities do not present themselves for critical examination to the public at large and do not make manifest their intentions, their methods, or their results to a society grown increasingly familiar with academic ways and increasingly amused by the foibles of the academy.

Colleges have utilized the college fair and hotel exhibition halls throughout the nation to sell their wares and deliver viewbooks, catalogs, and mementoes into the hands of prospective students, their parents, and their counselors. Radio and television daily popularize the results of research. But such exhibitions, while commonplace, fall far short of the openness to inquiry that is now required. I believe the new-found interest in marketing is a two-edged sword, in part calculated to circumvent and buffer legitimate inquiry. But in the view of some advocates it means taking a research-based approach to understanding the needs and aspirations of a diminishing pool of potential candidates and then determining honestly how best to serve them.

Dangers of Competitive Marketing

At a recent management institute sponsored by the New England Board of Higher Education and the New England Regional Office of

the College Board, Michael S. McPherson, a Williams College economist, raised some warning signals about the penchant for marketing in recruitment and admissions. "When everybody decides to
spend more on marketing," he said, "it's a little bit like everybody
showing up two hours early to get a good seat at the big game. Showing up early doesn't create any more seats. What happens is that
you wind up with everybody sitting two extra hours waiting for the
game to start in the same seat that they would have had anyway."
McPherson acknowledges that it is entirely legitimate to do a better job of informing prospective students about the processes of
higher education. But he worries about institutions' expenditures
of valuable and scarce resources that in his words "will ultimately
cancel each other out."[5]

The analogy of the multi-million dollar advertising campaigns
of competing companies with no benefit to the consumer is clear.
Colleges may be in danger of engaging in internecine recruiting
wars that absorb resources without alleviating the underlying
problems. The admissions officer of the future must have guts to
withstand the pressure to take more resources for promotion than
may be expended for academic advising or undergraduate tutorials.

The Williams College economist also warns us of the temptation
on the part of colleges to let tuition increases lag behind cost increases in order to compete with other institutions. Quality is
bound to suffer from such a practice. But the practitioners, in
McPherson's view, are hiding behind the awareness that the loss of
quality won't show up for several years. It's McPherson's contention that students would much prefer to cope with higher tuitions
than with programs of diminished quality. If students were taught
how to discern the relationship between cost and quality with the
help of the institutions they are considering, such an effort would
reflect a "marketing" approach that could be viewed as a public
service. It is unlikely to occur.

McPherson believes that "the institutions that are likely to succeed in the next decade are those which have both the strength and
the nerve to maintain their quality and charge the needed prices."

McPherson points out:

"We have the problem that everybody wants to be ten percent
larger at a time when the total number of clients is declining. In
fact, the Bowen and Minter report shows that most private institutions in 1977 actually projected being 15 percent larger in 1981 than
they are now. If a lot of private institutions are 15 percent larger in

a couple of years, a lot of other ones are going to be 100 percent smaller. This situation is rather like the gas shortage. The fear of rationing makes everyone fill their tanks, and that makes the shortage seem even worse. I think that attempts by all private institutions to grow will make the scramble for students even worse than it would be otherwise. It will lessen the possibility of a rational shakedown. As with the recruiting competition, it seems to me not at all obvious that the market on its own will achieve a sensible solution to these problems. One senses a need both for a certain amount of forbearance and farsightedness on the part of individual colleges to avoid this kind of destructive competition and also some broader measure of coordination at the system level."

These are enlightened cautionary words for us to bear in mind if we join the ranks of the marketers. And they should help us in our resolve to convert the unique problems of our era into an opportunity for improving the quality of our performance as educators. Too often, persons in educational leadership close their eyes and ears to the tidings of untoward trends. Glenny discussed this phenomenon in his contribution to *Higher Education: Myths, Realities, and Possibilities*. When he openly revealed to higher education leaders such trends as shrinking enrollments and the declining prestige of the college degree, the response of many state college and university presidents was one of "outright antagonism." Not, said Glenny, because they believed the trends to be unreal or invalidly interpreted but because "if public policymakers accept them as reality, the institutional goal to become an advanced graduate center is almost certain to be thwarted. Thus, the hard realities would be avoided, the policymakers deluded and, as in Greek times, the bearer of the bad tidings summarily executed."[6]

According to Glenny, one of the greatest myths of all is this: that as enrollments increase, programs produce more graduates, and unit costs go down. He cites several studies that indicate that the number of students enrolled in a program — taking courses and using the resources — has little relationship to the number of graduates from the program.[7]

One study conducted at Berkeley by David Breneman found that in a given period it took an average of 5.4 student years to produce a doctorate in chemistry, 8.6 years in history, 10.7 in political science, and 18.8 years in philosophy.[8] Such findings make clear the importance of research as the basis for any marketing ventures on the part of educators.

Influences of Consumerism

We are all familiar with the forces that have contrived to make higher education more consumer conscious and, at the same time, more marketing conscious. Again, there are those who react with uneasiness to such terms as product and customer, but who rejoice at the opportunity—indeed the requirement—now afforded to refine and improve, even as contraction occurs, the services provided students who are the consumers of higher education.

Prodded by students and by the federal government, educators are dealing energetically and, for the most part, wisely with consumerism. It has exposed, regrettably, a litany of past mistakes and areas of outright neglect. We have discovered that many of our procedures and publications have confused and misled college candidates, often resulting in poor decisions on their part about choice of college and program and in vast waste of precious faculty talent and human gifts.

As Elaine El-Khawas of ACE reminds us, we need to "take a thoughtful look at the underlying issues and to review our current procedures as they affect students. In principle," she says, "consumerism calls for an objective we all should share: honest publications and fair treatment of both prospective and enrolled students."[9]

This view receives hearty confirmation from leading campus publications. The pages of *CASE Currents*, the magazine of the Council for the Advancement and Support of Education, are replete with accounts of improved conditions on campus resulting from careful research and heightened communications characterized by increasing thoroughness and candor. Campuses are proud, as they should be, when they have found the means to express the truth.

College recruiting materials have all too frequently been slick publications proclaiming distinguished faculty, superior academic programs, stunning facilities, and renowned alumni. The discerning prospective student, in quest of the true picture, turned to underground literature or frank-talking students, or perhaps had an opportunity to audit classes and read the campus newspaper before enrolling. More often than not, the problems came more from omission than from misinformation or outright fraud, but the problems confronted by students seeking the best choice for themselves were real and pervasive nonetheless.

In this respect, colleges and universities have been helped enormously by the influential work of the National Task Force on Better Information for Student Choice. Supported by the Fund for the Improvement of Postsecondary Education of the U.S. Office of Education, the project was intended to help colleges develop candid and effective information for prospective students. According to Theodore J. Marchese, director of institutional research at Barat College (one of the participants), the prospectus Barat developed is "a document laying out the bad as well as the good and presenting in detail just what the prospective student is likely to find" at the college.[10]

The models prepared by the participating 11 colleges and 4 resource agencies (including the College Board) present the following types of information:

1. Up-to-date data on regional availability of jobs by career fields
2. Accurate educational cost projections (four years)
3. Description and explanation of student retention and attrition rates
4. Types of students who are most successful at the institution
5. Current student and faculty perceptions of the quality of teaching and learning
6. The extent and quality of student-faculty interactions
7. The environment of the campus as seen by various student subcultures and alumni
8. Assessment by alumni of the relationship between their educational experience and job advancement[11]

Obviously, it takes courage and discernment, as well as continuing research and communication, to produce an honest document. But we must summon that courage and discernment as we move beyond governmental decrees to deliver straightforward messages to the people we would like to serve. Such action from within can minimize if not deter arbitrary action by the government.

In responding to the pressure for more accurate information, many institutions are engaging legal counsel for opinions on liability with respect to published information — or misinformation. The body of legal opinion indicates that failure to deliver advertised or announced services is a breach of responsibility subject to legal action. We are all aware of, and sensitive to, the growing inclination of students and parents of students to take educators to court for not fulfilling contractual obligations.

It is not uncommon for those in education to view new legislation tied to consumerism as a threat to institutional autonomy. Accentuating the positive again, we might better view the phenomenon as encouragement to establish greater clarity and understanding in the public mind about the character, the processes, and the results of postsecondary education. Mandated or not, the pressure for more public disclosure can be seen as a blessing in disguise. It is in the national interest and in the academy's long-term interest that better information be developed and disseminated by institutions of higher learning. The effort serves to demystify academic administrative processes and the learned professions and to facilitate access to higher education for qualified and qualifiable citizens. In the past, access has been restricted by the severely limited information resources of reliable quality available to all prospective students. Let us hope that we have entered an era when it would be impossible for Abraham Flexner to write, as he did in 1932, that "American universities . . . go into the marketplace and do a thriving business with the mob. They advertise their shoddy wares in newspapers and periodicals. . . . Many of the activities carried on by numerous universities are little short of dishonest; but the business goes on, because it pays — for that and for no other reason."[12]

As I have observed elsewhere, each assertion made in a publication should be supported by current data based on institutional research or informed self-assessment. Care must be taken not to overwhelm an applicant with statistics in the guise of providing objective facts. Information should be provided about the encouraging or limiting (positive and negative) aspects of an institution when these statistics are known. Whenever possible, information should be comparative. Admissions standards, financial aid allocations, graduate professional school admissions data, and career information can be presented comparatively, when such information as part of a substantive approach to marketing has been carefully gathered. Though few institutions currently acknowledge they possess such data, government regulations now require they be proclaimed. Although that requirement has not yet been fully enforced, I would suggest it be honored rapidly.

Difficulties indeed exist in providing comparative data to prospective students, largely because of the absence of shared standardized information or even a common vocabulary among institutions of similar type. In the future, institutions will find it necessary to share comparative data, which in turn will be used by the public. The language of a new information vehicle must be scrutinized to ensure clarity and readability and to avoid the time-worn cliches, educational jargon, and dedicated obscurity characteristic of the collegiate catalog. Ventures that encourage institutions to co-operate in providing joint publications have been few and far between, but I predict such efforts will abound by 1990.

While the availability of good information does not guarantee wise use by prospective students (or for that matter, administrators), it should at least reduce the extent of student distrust and the costly mismatches that occur when poorly informed students choose a college or a program that does not suit their needs. Both college and student interests are served when the information provided leads to mutually predictable expectations. The credibility of a college will be enhanced if it responds voluntarily and effectively to consumer needs.

At the heart of the consumer movement is the demand that institutions reveal how they have measurably influenced the intellectual development of students and the attainment of specific competencies. What in essence does the undergraduate receive for that $10,000 unrestricted gift? In addition there is a demand for the development of a new awareness of the relationship of intellect, competence, and values in making personal and professional decisions. In the light of these expectations, colleges and universities must be alert to their own very specific strengths and weaknesses in contributing to students' intellectual development, their search for values, and their attainment of competencies. What are the attitudes of faculty and administration on questions of significance? Clearly, students must be full partners in such an inquiry and not passive subjects for analysis. As I observed in 1976: "Understanding and responding to students' needs and *aspirations* may very soon become a *primary* goal of higher education instead of a tertiary one."[13] In retrospect, that seems to have been a safe prediction.

Honesty in leaders is placed at a premium by a public grown highly skeptical in the 1970s. A new pecking order will be established on the ladder of candor and institutional self-knowledge in the 1980s. As exercised by institutional leadership, forthrightness can help significantly in the arduous climb back to a level of stature that inspires confidence anew in the educational enterprise by the public.

The Role of the Admissions Officer
In the past, and understandably so, faculty have given more at-

tention to the concerns of their own disciplines than to the broader concerns and needs of the institution they serve or of higher education generally. Today, however, faculty appear prepared to exhibit increasing concern for the welfare of the student as consumer. Student-affairs personnel used to see themselves as lonely student advocates, and admissions offices were left pretty much to their own devices. There was a danger here of losing sight of institutional priorities through specialization. What is needed is a perspective reflecting the higher interests of the college, based on a coalition of campus interests rather than a reinforcement of old-time divisions on campus. Those who will be responsible for the enrollment process must be able to work with, indeed inspire confidence in, the faculty. Perhaps the single most important quality in the admissions officer of the 1980s will be the ability to explain to and encourage participation in the admissions process by faculty members, including those both supportive and critical. Marketing, if we are to have a major flirtation with it in higher education, must in fact begin at home with the faculty.

The admissions office, or as it is called in some meetings, the enrollment office or the office of relations with schools, will require vigorous leadership and integrity in the 1980s. The officer of this mission will be in a position to profoundly influence the destiny of any campus in the nation in the course of the next decade. Admissions officers must possess the skills to fully utilize available information and generate the kind of data needed to foster thorough institutional analysis and understanding of campus realities. Far too few campuses emphasize the analytical skills necessary to be qualified as a member of the admissions staff. Especially on a small campus the admissions officer plays a crucial role in assisting the president, the board, and the faculty in understanding the reality base the institution must establish.

Most institutions will assign the admissions task to an experienced individual with sufficient background to run a steady, efficient, and responsive communications-oriented program. If an institution has a specialist in gimmickry heading the admissions office — an administrator given to techniques aimed at controlling the wheel of fortune — he or she should be summarily dismissed. The decade ahead will be a serious affair; dalliance with superficial and clever techniques will fail. Even without the help of marketing consultants, the promoting of success through attention-getting devices was threatening to become a fine art in higher education.

In any event, such approaches will become wide open to ridicule as the education editor of the *New York Times* has already revealed to those who are tempted.

Most presidents will seriously consider having the director of admissions report directly to themselves, if this is not already the case. It is interesting to note that in the most selective institutions in the nation, this is nearly always the pattern and has been so for several decades. However, for a variety of reasons some presidents may wish to place the admissions office under the dean of the faculty or the vice president for administration, providing distance between themselves and the enrollment issue. Such placement must be accompanied by a thoughtful and accurate plan, or the president may awaken to a crisis over which little control can be exercised.

In the 1980s the admissions office may lose a number of the functions that have historically resided within the structure of a comprehensive admissions office including:

- Alumni volunteer participation
- Processing of applications in favor of "recruitment" activities
- Publications
- Financial aid (first-time awards)
- Responsibility for faculty liaison and policy recommendations

A variety of pressures on the admissions office will *decrease* on most campuses. Among these will be:

- Scrutiny of selective criteria
- Alumni legacy issues on acceptance/rejection
- Political pressure on acceptance/rejection
- Inadequate budget support
- Publications development support
- Reluctance on the part of the alumni, faculty, and administration to assist
- Disseminating adequate information on enrollment analysis requiring effort to get the campus to pay attention
- Negotiations related to distributing financial aid resources
- More time on campus

Conversely, pressures that will *increase* are related to all of the above:

- Scrutiny of nonselective criteria
- Alumni overly interested in being helpful (requiring continuing communication)
- Political interest in how the campus is doing on a comparative

basis

- Scrutiny of the utilization and effective deployment of resources
- Intense discussion requiring negotiations about the presentation of the campus in publications
- Intense faculty interest in being helpful requiring consultant attention
- Requests for information related to enrollment trends requiring careful response
- Careful monitoring of external and internal requests for information concerning adequacy of financial aid resources
- Organizing campus-based resources in order to free staff to be on the road visiting schools
- Analysis of the productive use of staff time in the field
- Expansion of the role of professional associations and consortia requiring a greater level of representation than in the past and the delegation of such responsibility beyond the admissions office itself
- Involvement of campus leaders including the president, vice presidents, and deans in "appropriate" enrollment-related programs
- Level of responsiveness to media, campus newspapers, and service organizations requiring information and a sense of attentiveness
- Personalization of direct contact with prospective students and their parents

The irony of this partial sketch of pressure-related activities is the assumption that higher education has been operating in a vacuum, riding out demographic trends with such ease that it has neglected market factors over the past four decades.

Conclusion

The expansion of higher education in America has, if we chose to describe it in such terms, been a marketing phenomenon. There is presumptive arrogance in suggesting at the point where demography turns against us that scientific marketing will now solve our problem. The point is that our processes may not have done the complete job — but I for one do not see any other unit in the American economy that has done as well as fruitfully and as consistently in recent decades.

In New England the region's colleges and universities are the cutting edge of the economy itself. Higher education is the principal business of the New England economy. Followed by electronics and service industries, higher education is a regional, national, and international economic resource. It has attained this preeminent position as the major element in the knowledge-intensive industry of the region through a series of sophisticated and responsive processes of its own. Indeed, higher education, poised on the brink of so-called demographic disaster, may actually be in a position to provide a significant analysis of the factors that have permitted it to cope with the most powerful bulge in the demography of this nation in its entire history.

A demographic phenomenon has just moved to the marketplace of the economy of jobs. This new generation of Americans has been well schooled in the preoccupation of business selling to them as teenagers. They are sophisticated enough and educated enough to be capable of sending the automobile industry, the housing market, the entertainment business, and the advertising media back to the drawing boards.

Make no mistake about this assertion. For the past 20 years, higher education in America has responded to the aspirations of its young people. With brute strength and awkwardness, the academy has attempted to provide unprecedented numbers of young Americans with a modest degree of critical instruction. They have with the audacity of youth instructed us. They have survived our instruction, our ineptness, and our confusion. They are now the adults of the nation, and the marketing experts will have to learn how to deal with them. They will be tough, for the sixties and seventies were tough decades in which to grow up.

I frankly do not know what their values as adults will be. I do not know what to expect of them. They have been generally quite unpredictable, and I trust this dimension will soften a bit; but not too much, for it is clear that the market economy of this nation needs a few jolts from an ascendant and critical group of citizens. The young will soon have enough economic clout to redefine how they are marketed to by business and industry.

I believe these young men and women, unprecedented in numbers, will reflect credit on the higher education system from whence they sprang. I look forward to their criticism as citizens, their concern as consumers, and their priorities as they assume responsibility as our next generation of leaders and policy makers.

In the interim, I suspect we will, with their help, learn how to handle the demographics of decline. If we put it up, we can, as the saying goes, take it down again.

Before we do, it may be worth analyzing the extent to which we know more than we care to admit, and perhaps more than our colleagues outside of education, about the needs of people and how to reach them in flush times, and potentially I might add, in thin.

References

1. Lyman Glenny, "Diversification and Quality Control," pp. 3-19 in *Higher Education: Myths, Realities, and Possibilities*, Winfred L. Godwin and Peter B. Mann, editors. Atlanta, Ga.: Southern Regional Education Board, 1972.

2. David W. Barton, Jr., "Student Population," CASE *Currents*, February 1976, p. 30.

3. Dennis L. Johnson, "Marketing the 'UN-COLA' College," *Community and Junior College Journal*, Vol. 48, No. 4, December/January 1977-78, p. 15.

4. Ibid., p. 16.

5. Michael S. McPherson, "Higher Education: Value and Demand," Management Seminar for College and University Presidents, Chief Academic Officers, Deans and Directors of Admissions, Boxborough, Mass., March 5, 1979 (in press).

6. Glenny, "Diversification," p. 9.

7. Ibid., p. 15.

8. Ibid.

9. Elaine El-Khawas, "Consumerism Comes to Campus," *CASE Currents*, February 1976, p. 5.

10. John C. Hoy, "Your Campus, Warts and All," *CASE Currents*, March 1977, p. 12.

11. Ibid. John C. Hoy, "Consumer Interest in Higher Education," *Educational Record*, Vol. 58, No. 2, 1977, pp. 182-184.

12. Abraham Flexner, "University in American Life," *Atlantic Monthly*, September 1932, p. 626.

13. John C. Hoy, "A Question of Balance," *College Board Review*, No. 101, Fall 1976, p. 7.

Marketing Perspectives: Student and National Interests

By Stephen K. Bailey

The initiative of AACRAO, NACAC, and the College Board in calling
this conference (with the gracious assistance of the Johnson Foundation) is both commendable and courageous: commendable because the issues are important; courageous because there is no
a priori reason for assuming that student interests and national
interests are automatically served by admissions officers pursuing
perceived self-interests or the interests of their respective institutions. Adam Smith's "unseen hand" may indeed, in this instance,
be iron-fisted and sinister. The predominant effect of a shrinking
college market may well be to elicit the tawdriest of business competitive compulsions — especially the three self-protective admonitions: cut rates, cut corners, and cut throats. The only deference to
conscience may well be reiterated Darwinian allusions justifying
any and all competitive practices on the grounds of "survival of the
fittest" — pushing into unremembrance the wisdom that questions
whether those fit to survive are in truth fit for anything else.

Competition Is Not New

Competition for students is hardly a new collegiate phenomenon.
In fact, for some of us, current discussions bring forth an enormous
sense of deja vu. My first academic job was as director of admissions at Hiram College in the year 1940-41. Eleven months before
Pearl Harbor, on a bitterly cold January day, I found myself setting up my brochures, flyers, calendars, catalogs, and application
forms in the basement cafeteria of the Warren Harding High
School in Warren, Ohio. Two college-bound seniors were graduating
mid-year. Fifty — count 'em, 50 — Ohio, Pennsylvania, and West
Virginia colleges and universities had display desks and admissions
officers in that cafeteria on that cold winter's day — 50 salesmen
after 2 bewildered prospects who must have completed their tour
of displays with enormously enhanced egos. I do not remember
what I said when asked by the two students how Hiram compared
with, say, Mt. Union, Denison, Oberlin, or Kent State. I hope I
presaged your recently published code of ethics and put Hiram's
best foot forward without landing it on the rear end of the competitors. But there were then, as there are now, gentle ways of doing
this. "Oh, you are interested in serious music? Hiram has an ex-

cellent music department. Kent State? Well, I understand that Kent State has a fine marching band."

Even in the halcyon days of our immediate past, competition for students—especially student athletes, particularly *black* student athletes—has been commonplace. And first priority was not always given to academic virtuosity. Many of us remember as prototypical the story of the football coach at a major state university who wanted to hire (excuse me, recruit) a talented pass receiver whose SAT math scores matched his weight at around 230. The admissions officer referred the case to a math professor who was, as Joe Nyquist has put it, a warm athletic supporter. The math professor decided that the matter of admissions would be determined by asking the recruit one question in arithmetic: "How much is seven and seven?" The hapless jock strained and strained and finally blurted out, "seventeen." The math professor sadly turned thumbs down. The coach remonstrated, "Gee whiz, Prof, he only missed it by two."

In sum, competition for students is not new. What is new are the demographic projections of the next decade, which, it is believed by many, will set the climate for a kind of competitive orgy. At the end of this road, to borrow some bitter imagery from Clark Kerr, is an academy that has become one huge used-car lot.

Others at this conference have described and analyzed the unsettling demographic trends of the 1980s. I would only reemphasize that the aggregate national projections are too sanguine by half for some kinds of colleges and universities in some geographic areas; overly and unnecessarily scary for others. As ACE's Cathy Henderson has pointed out, admissions officers in Arizona are not likely to face the same trouble as those at a liberal arts college or a rurally based state institution in Pennsylvania or New York. Furthermore, most prospective college students will do a lot less shopping around than many marketing strategies assume. Factors of status, friends, parental pressures, convenience, and cost will continue to drive most college-bound toward institutions they deem appropriate to their own circumstances. Harvard is not directly competitive with Miami-Dade Community College. Wisconsin natives aspiring to Stanford are unlikely to be attracted to Oral Roberts. Only a fraction (some would place that at 10 percent or less) of the prospective student population is in a truly competitive pool—and even in that fraction the competitive market tends to be controlled by a few institutions (what economists, I believe, call "oligopoly") rather than by "free" market forces in classical economic terms. Sophisticated market analysts know all this, but the untutored pitch-person can waste untold resources casting about in applicant pools that are either unstocked or where the lure is totally inappropriate.

Under such imperfect market conditions, all that can be achieved is to make prospects, parents, and politicians cynical and angry when fancy four-color brochures and mechanically "personalized" letters from one hundred different colleges cascade into the mailboxes of all high school seniors, the upper half of the junior class, and the upper third of tenth graders; or when instructors inflate grades to attract large classes. (I learned recently of a part-time instructor who gleefully reported to a friend of mine that by giving all A's he was thereby assured of a big class next year.) Such hucksterism and such perversions can only bring down public support for higher education as a serious academic enterprise. It is not that the academy will totally crumble under the present avalanche of market surveys, Madison Avenue ploys, and soft standards. But gradually the academy's traditional class system will become more marked as the patently meretricious hawk their wares with indiscriminate abandon and the elite 10 percent of the academy savor the tangibles and intangibles of selectivity. The dignity and the responsibility of the total higher education enterprise will suffer. I cannot believe that, in the long range, tarnished academic hallmarks are in the interest of students, the public at large, or the institutions themselves. It is this theme that will dominate my remarks on this occasion. I hope to convince you that the present market competition is a handmaiden to a headlong flight from academic rigor and responsibly fashioned curriculum structures – and that this trend is ultimately disastrous to students and to the nation. The trend must be stopped.

The Counterargument

I begin, however, with a counterargument. It is that we are presently playing out the ultimate logic of a system that long ago cast itself adrift from the moorings of traditional academic pretensions. It is argued that higher education once – and not so many decades ago – catered largely to a tiny minority of rich and fortunate. It was designed to cultivate gentlemen and train a limited number of professionals. The gentlemen got C's, the preprofessionals got A's and B's. The great majority of late teenagers never went to college at all. They were in the labor force or were unemployed – having dropped out of school somewhere between grades 6 and 13.

Then came the GI Bill, the postwar baby boom, and the rise in economic and social expectations of the larger citizenry. College became an economic possibility and a status magnet for multitudes. In the sixties and seventies, state and federal aid featured equal educational opportunity – equal opportunity ambiguously defined to include both life chances and symbolic rewards.

Under these pressures, higher education changed its basic mission. Its social utility had increasingly little to do with the honing of minds and the perfecting of talents. Instead, colleges and universities came to provide a series of valued custodial and diversionary functions. The higher academy became a holding vat for young people – keeping them out of a soft labor market. It was a place where adolescents could, for certain hours of the day or months in the year, find escape from parental authority – simultaneously providing parents with some escape from adolescent hostility and insolence. Colleges and universities became socializing instruments – introducing young people to a pluralistic peer society. They provided young people with harmless, sometimes even useful diversions – bowling, swimming, beer and pot parties, rallies, spectator sports, plays, music festivals, dances. And all of these took place within an environment marked by the symbols, accoutrements, traditions, and finally awards associated historically with higher learning. What conceivable difference could it make if the old ideals of rigorous intellectual training, of scholarship, of academic excellence, were eroded? Have not these ancient standards, except in a chosen few institutions, become archaic?

Colleges and universities have assumed other socially valued roles, and these roles are by and large sufficiently removed from traditional canons of learning to make questions of academic competence – either for admission or for retention and graduation – totally irrelevant. In such a world, competitive huckstering for what are euphemistically still referred to as students (the proper term is probably "attendees") is as legitimate as competitive huckstering for military service, for stereo-sound equipment, for tapes and records, or for discos and restaurants. A valued service is promised, but the service is largely diversionary in an egalitarian environment rather than intellectually rigorous in a meritrocratic environment. Hence, open admissions, grade inflation, gigantic deans' lists, and the endless proliferation of certificates, programs, and degrees. But in a sense, it is argued, everybody wins: society has created a midway and a holding vat for youth, so the national economy is served; attendees enjoy useful diversions and receive honored certificates and degrees of proven past utility in the worlds of jobs and status; faculty and administrators have generally respected and reasonably secure employment; admissions officers can legitimately concentrate on bodies not on minds and, like carnival barkers, can play any tricks of seduction that do not offend customer sensibilities.

Whatever caricature is involved in the above, who can doubt that some parts of the system do in fact operate as though such assumptions were in effect? What if anything is wrong with such a scenario? What student interests, what national interests, are in point of fact violated? Again, these are the key issues of this paper.

The Trivialization of Learning

Before trying to address these questions, let me complicate the problem by adding a complementary dimension to contemporary academic practice: what might be called the trivialization of learning in the name of customer convenience and career relevance. In my monograph *Academic Quality Control: The Case of College Programs on Military Bases,* I cited some disturbing examples of academic offerings and practices that provided military personnel with the shadow of academic respectability but not with its substance.[1] These examples have been put in a larger context by the Carnegie Council in its book *Fair Practices.*[2] More recently, Frank Wolf, an associate dean at Columbia University, wrote an op-ed piece for the *New York Times* on what was going on in academia in the name of "lifelong learning."[3]

He abstracted 16 examples from a larger list of 350 suggestions collected and published by the College Board.[4] The following are the 16 Wolf cited:

"1. State in advertisements that you will develop a class for any 15 people interested in a particular subject.

"2. In deciding what courses to offer, try to identify what books people are borrowing from the local library and what shows they are watching on television.

"3. Develop undergraduate and graduate degrees with no on-campus requirements.

"4. Offer a mini-course on emergency medical procedures for ambulance drivers.

"5. Develop special courses for widows and divorcees.

"6. Offer packages that include charter flights and combine vacations in foreign countries with courses for credit.

"7. Seek instructors for distance learning courses who do not mind a lack of personal contact with students, as most give-and-take is by mail.

"8. Rent billboard space in key locations and advertise, 'If it is education service you want, call us.'

"9. Set up booths in shopping malls with posters, slides and representatives to describe your program.

"10. Remove limits to the amount of credit that can be earned by examination.

"11. Increase the amount of credit granted for off-campus experiential learning.

"12. Allow noncredit courses to be taken for credit through negotiations with the department head and professor.

"13. Establish storefront posts staffed by professional counselors to advise drop-ins about career and educational needs and opportunities.

"14. Create a lottery sponsored by a public or private organization with one prize: free enrollment in your program.

"15. Overload popular courses to cover the costs of those that attract fewer than the minimum number of registrants.

"16. Establish a policy that when courses do not cover their costs in any one year, they will not be offered the following year."[5]

Frank Wolf concludes from this litany, "These are 16 ways to destroy a university."[6] He might have added another: advertise all courses as job specific and label the liberal arts as useless, archaic elitism. I do not happen to believe in a universal liberal-arts theology. The new Harvard College requirements are a useful "for instance," but they are not carved in stone, and I happen to quarrel with some of their sins of omission. On the other hand, to settle for a college fare that is *only* job oriented—especially first job oriented—seems to me a massive perversion of the functions of higher education.

As I pointed out in my book *The Purposes of Education*,[7] if we live to be 80 we will have lived 700,000 hours. Knock off a couple of hundred-thousand hours for sleep, we still have a half-million hours of waking existence. Of that number only 90,000 hours—less than one-fifth of the total—will be spent by people on a remunerated job. What in God's name will people do with the other 410,000 hours of their life? As my friend Jack Arbolino is fond of putting it, the reason for liberal arts is so that later on in life when you knock on yourself, somebody answers.

At the heart of liberal learning are the disciplined uses of verbal and symbolic language, the understanding of the inner world of the human psyche, a sense of spatial and historic context and relationship, an awareness of civility and community, and an appreciation of the lasting satisfaction associated with the best that the aesthetic and spiritual geniuses of the race have produced. To remove such concerns from the center of college and university programs is to trivialize further the academic experience and to diminish the hopes and aspirations of the human race.

Here then are the two great rationalizations for slovenliness in academic marketing:

1. The emerging egalitarian, nonacademic social purposes of higher education.

2. The trivialization of learning that stems from the contemporary saliency of customer convenience and job hunger.

An Ideal Model

Why are long-term student and national interests seriously eroded by such developments?—for I most deeply believe that they are.

To answer this question, it seems to me important to repair to what many would consider to be an ideal model of a college or university. I am aware that this leads me onto dangerous grounds. Cardinal Newman is not Frank Newman. Berkeley is not Slippery Rock. The classical traditions epitomized in the Yale Report of 1828 are in many ways a far cry from the visions of Justin Smith Morrill in 1862. Nonetheless, there are some root expectations at the core of the higher education traditions in this country. These include, it seems to me, at least the following:

First, that instructional staffs are marked by experience, academic record, and earned degrees as having met the approval of highly qualified peers.

Second, that a curriculum is a considered intellectual structure with some semblance of a core requirement in liberal learning—not just a smorgasbord of disparate courses or a demand-driven set of subject-matter-specific, career-oriented training modules.

Third, that support systems such as libraries, laboratories, computer services, and audiovisual aids are adequately financed and staffed to support the curriculum and the various levels and modes of instruction.

Fourth, that students are prepared by previous scholastic and academic accomplishments and by motivation to enter into and profit from truly advanced learning.

Fifth, that the evaluation of a student's intellectual progress is assumed to relate to the quality of academic performance — merit measured by proximations to high standards of knowledge and skill established by disciplinary and professional experts.

Sixth, that by tenure agreements or collective-bargaining contracts, the professoriat are protected against job insecurity or other harassments triggered by what they say or write — and that this atmosphere of academic freedom suffuses the intellectual and social life of the student.

There may be other common hallmarks of the higher academy at its best, but these at least seem to me central. Normatively, they are as true for community colleges as for elite universities. But, so stated, the propositions are unashamedly meritrocratic. The instructional staffs are not picked up off the street; they must have demonstrated high levels of intellectual, technical, or aesthetic competence to their peers. Curriculums are not slap-dash listings of academic whims; they are a studied ordering of intellectual priorities and sequences — implying that some courses and programs are more meritorious than others. Support systems are not for show but for carefully defined intellectual utility. Students, no matter how equal before God and the law, are bright enough and well enough prepared, and sufficiently highly motivated, to make reasonable use of the high-priced faculties and facilities that comprise modern universities and colleges. "College bred" does not mean a lot of dough for a four-year loaf, but demonstrated knowledge and skills of a high order for which one is rewarded with suitable grades, credits, and degrees.

The Clear and Present Danger

Assuming that this ideal has never existed in a pure and pristine form, is its studied approximation in the national interest and in the interest of students? Put another way, when we lose sight of this lodestar, are we in danger of making a mockery of the collegiate and university experience?

The dangers are most clearly exemplified in learned professions like medicine and engineering. Let us assume that engineers and doctors could receive their advanced degrees on the basis of policies of open admission, casual attendance in class, and inflated grades. I submit that the national interest would be jeopardized, the whole system of professional licensure would break down, and individual students would be seriously hampered in their struggle for professional advancement. Malpractice suits would mushroom, and the holding of a professional degree would become meaningless.

Moving to the graduate disciplines in arts and sciences, the social damage would be less immediate and cataclysmic. But the whole fabric of scholarship would ultimately become unraveled. The patiently built structures of method and substance would collapse into a jelly. No peer groups would exist to license pretenders to the mortar board and gown. Undergraduate instruction would gradually lose its authority and excitement.

The tragedy is that such distressing downward effects have their precise parallels in *upward* effects. Make carefully and highly trained professors deal with undergraduate students who are unequipped intellectually and uninspired motivationally, and you set loose a series of predictable consequences. The professoriat has no instructional challenge, so its own canons of proof and its own clarity of exposition begin to lose their edge. Tough-minded grading leads to a drop in class enrollments. This in an enrollment-driven and decremental-budgeting world leads to questions of job security. Incentives exist to "go easy." Bright and highly motivated students become cynical as the indolent and the dull receive the same grades and credentials as they. Graduate schools then admit these cynical and improperly trained students, and a similar dry rot begins to infuse graduate programs—disciplinary and professional. Traditional standards begin to collapse all over the place. The nation becomes peopled by academic and professional "Kentucky colonels."

We are not there yet—thank God!—but this is the road we are traveling. In the name of equality, consumer service, career relevance, institutional survival, and marketing strategies, we are in the process of undermining the temple of learning in this nation. I cannot believe that this is the long-range interest either of individual students or of the nation as a whole. To use a Biblical allusion that is fast becoming recondite, we are selling our souls for a mess of pottage.

What Is to Be Done?

The question is, of course, what is to be done? One plausible answer is nothing. One can make the argument that what has been set in motion is inexorable. The process of decay is endemic, originating in the shortcomings of primary and secondary education, in parental neglect and permissiveness, and in television. These baneful forces are simply exacerbated by interinstitutional competition for live enrollments and increased retentions. Furthermore, certain egalitarians might contend that nothing *should* be done. Their argument could well be that there is no way of tightening academic standards significantly across the board without denying the traditionally deprived in our midst of a chance to enter or to receive the ultimate certificates, heraldry, and privileges associated with college and university experience. It might be argued further that there have always been, and presumably will continue to be, a small number of elite institutions (the Ivy League; the M.I.T.s, Michigans, Wisconsins, and Cal Techs; the Swarthmores, Amhersts, Carletons, Bowdoins, and Vassars) that make a fetish of standards and will supply the nation with a sufficient cadre of top professional and technical personnel in the years ahead to keep the reputations of these elevated endeavors brightly burnished. But for the rest of the system — the less famous land-grant institutions, the state colleges, the less illustrious private universities, the less prestigious liberal arts colleges, and above all the community colleges — let them do their own useful, if academically tawdry, thing. To paraphrase Emma Lazarus:

Give me your mired, your poor,
Your befuddled masses yearning for a degree,
The wretched refuse of your teenage horde.
Send these, the feckless, SAT-lost to me,
I'll give them a degree for their room and board.

From some vantage points, this is a plausible — perhaps inevitable — scenario. But is it in the long-range interest of the nation and of individual students? Is it really in the national or student interest to promote an even more rigid class society than we now have? — a society that says to the Stanford or Williams graduate, "You are among Plato's philosopher kings with all of the rights and privileges thereunto pertaining; you are the mandarins of the future"; but says to the graduate of North Dakota State and Miami-Dade Community College: "Be satisfied with artisanship and soldiery, for that is all to which your college education entitles and enables you to aspire."

Is it really in either the national interest or student interest for students to be told that their degrees are worthless apart from a prospective employer's knowledge of where a particular degree is from? For if degrees lose their power as a respected medium of exchange, if academic inflation does to a B.A. or an M.A. what economic inflation did to the reichsmark in the early 1920s, why should anyone invest in such shoddy paper?

The opposite scenario is quite as gloomy — and even more unrealistic: all colleges and universities accept a popular caricature of admissions criteria of Harvard and Stanford. Admissions officers take an informed risk with a few — very few — deprived ethnics and a few jocks, but generally colleges and universities set combined SAT scores near the 1400 mark. Admissions becomes a virtual guarantor of graduation. Under these circumstances, of course, three quarters or more of our institutions of higher education would go out of business. The nation's class system would become even more dangerously polarized. Youth unemployment and restlessness would skyrocket. A lot of people would live out lives substantially more impoverished than they do today.

There is a third scenario. It holds long-range promise, but it promises no quick fix. It is, I believe, based in contemporary reality. If dutifully pursued, it could enable us to hold our heads high. It seems to me to be in the interest of both individual students and the nation as a whole.

The scenario is that starting immediately college and university leaders begin to work with K through 12 education leaders in elevating the standards of elementary and secondary schooling in this nation. Part of this elevation would take the form of special scholarship incentives for pupils who do well consistently over the course of their scholastic careers or who make dramatic improvements in performance during their high school years. The twelfth grade would increasingly become a swing year during which superior high school performance is awarded college credit.

With this as background, the testing industry would work with admissions people in developing a battery of differentiated tests that would go far beyond the SAT in meeting the various quantitative and qualitative indexes needed by particular colleges and universities as guides to admission to their various programs.

Community-wide, professionally staffed educational brokering services, not tied to any one institution, but endorsed by all of the major higher education institutions in an area, would come to permeate the landscape. There, any individual of any age or previous condition of intellectual servitude could go for expert advice on the facilities, programs, standards, and costs of institutions judged by the prospective student to be plausibly related to his or her condition. If test scores indicate that a higher education institution requires standards of performance beyond a prospective student's present level of achievement, preentry remedial programs would be available at local high schools, regional intermediate schools, and/or community colleges — using the latest in computerized, auto-instructional, and audiovisual technology.

Accrediting bodies — regional, professional, and state — would increase their surveillance of academic shoddiness and of cutthroat and undignified competitive practices, and would publicize each year a black list of those who refuse to improve their ways.

State higher education planning, coordinating, and governing bodies would do everything in their power to find funding formulas that reward accretions in an institution's academic quality rather than enrollments. For example, two percent improvement in student performances on differentiated regional or national (but not federal) tests would be worth an extra two million dollars in state institutional aid. Each student would receive an extra amount above the regular BEOG and SEOG allotment for superior performance on such standardized tests. Institutions of higher education willing to accept outside examiners as the arbiters of student honors grades (as Oxford and Swarthmore have done for years) would receive special dispensations in state and federal allotments. Increasingly differentiated grading curves would be similarly rewarded.

Fundamental to all such changes would be the establishment within each institution of a prestigious committee on academic quality comprised of faculty and admissions officers. This committee would examine all parts of the institution's curriculum and services, including its entrance and retention policies, and make periodic recommendations to the faculty senate and to the administration of ways and means to improve academic standards.

I need not go on. All of you, I am sure, see the general draft of the scenario I am trying to construct and that I urgently recommend. No one will pretend that it would be easy to accomplish. In some ways it is to unbridled marketing competition and academic inflation what cold turkey is to drug abuse, what a Pritikin diet is to the obese, or what stringent deflationary policies are to a bloated economy. In the short run it could be disruptive, unnerving, and in some cases punitive to classes of students and to marginal institutions alike. But something like it is imperative if we are to rediscover the essentiality of standards to the long-range health of our academic life, and if we are to stop carving each other up in the name of egalitarianism, consumer convenience, careerism, and sophisticated marketing strategies.

The Gospel according to St. Mark said it all: "For what shall it profit a man, if he shall gain the whole world, and lose his own soul?"

References

1. Washington, D.C.: American Association for Higher Education, 1979.

2. Carnegie Council on Policy Studies in Higher Education, Fair Practices in Higher Education. San Francisco: Jossey-Bass, Inc., Publishers, 1979.

3. "Hey, Getcher Savwor Fare—Red Hot!" New York Times, August 21, 1979, p. A19.

4. Future Directions for a Learning Society, 350 Ways Colleges Are Serving Adult Learners. New York: College Entrance Examination Board, 1979.

5. Wolf, "Savwor Fare."

6. Ibid.

7. Bloomington, Ind.: Phi Delta Kappa Educational Foundation, 1976.

Marketing, the Public Interest, and the Production of Social Benefits in Higher Education

by Douglas M. Windham

Introduction

In the next two decades higher education in the United States will undergo a period of unprecedented decline in the demand for instructional services. As has been pointed out, the most common institutional reaction to this threat will be an increased use of marketing to attract students. This paper will examine specifically what the relationship is between the new demographics of higher education demand, the practice of marketing, and the production of those social benefits that have long been the primary rationale for public support of higher education. Is the public interest in higher education threatened by the evolving orientation toward student interests in the administration of the higher education system?

If one depended upon the popular press for one's information, it would appear that the imminent decline in the traditional demographic base of supply of students for higher education has led to a sudden discovery by the American universities and colleges of the concept of marketing. However, to anyone with more than a passing familiarity with the history and structure of American higher education, the current behavior of these institutions is only a new stage in a long-term trend toward increased student control or influence upon the structure of their education. Higher education has, of course, always been characterized by marketing in the nonpejorative sense: the elite institutions marketed a specific image of "quality" so as to attract the intellectual and financial elite; religiously oriented colleges put forth a blend of academic and moral-ethical training; and local institutions sold themselves more on a basis of convenience and economy than on excellence.

Beyond this recognition of the advantages of market differentiation, few institutions before the 1970s needed to concern themselves with the question of institutional survival and marketing as a means thereto. However, many institutions did respond to the student protests of the 1960s by removing or reducing much of the required structure of the student curriculum. Regardless of the justification for these changes, they may be viewed as "marketing" effects because of the need perceived by the administration and faculty to mollify student disaffection to maintain enrollments. Further evidence of the entrepreneurial nature of this response can be seen in the institutions' willingness to reinstitute requirements once students began to meet with a reduced employment demand for graduates of the less-structured curricula.

The current condition of marketing in higher education is characterized by a historically unique phenomenon, the real prospect of market failure, i.e., the closing of institutions. Under this threat, the traditional diversity of higher education has been increased. The difficulty for institutions has been exacerbated by increased competition from the rest of the postsecondary education industry and especially by the expansion of nontraditional higher education programs requiring reduced, and in some cases no, campus residency. The result has been an increasing hysteria on the part of marginal higher education institutions. They have engaged in a variety of activities (misleading catalogs, credit giveaways, front-loaded financial aid, etc.) that are reprehensible not because they represent marketing, but because they represent unethical if not illegal activities. Meanwhile, the vast majority of institutions have engaged in more traditional marketing strategies, emphasizing greater dissemination of information and increased institutional specialization. Both of these actions may be seen as attempts by an individual college or university to differentiate itself from the mass of potential institutions to which a student may apply.

Within this historical and institutional context this paper will analyze the nature of the social benefits of higher education, the relevance of social benefits to public subsidization of higher education, the probable effects of the current marketing phenomenon upon production of social benefits, and the evolving rationale for the continued public responsibility to higher education. For this analysis to be useful, however, one must begin with a brief exploration of the competitive market for higher education in the United States.

The Higher Education Market

Higher education, for the purpose of this discussion, will be restricted to predominantly campus-based programs of study leading to a baccalaureate or equivalent degree. Although this excludes a wide variety of vocational programs offered in two-year institutions, it does include academic transfer programs offered by the community college systems in the various states. Even with the above restrictions, higher education remains varied by such crucial considerations as perceived quality, size, location, program specializations, and of course, costs. In fact, it makes more sense to view the higher education industry as characterized by a network of separate sectors drawing on different markets that overlap only slightly.

Most visible are the prestige private institutions that attract a national student body from a distinct market. Second are the high quality public institutions that have evolved in the last two decades into competitors for the national student market even though they draw primarily from their own state applicants. Third would be those private and public institutions that have developed strong program specializations and draw from a regional student pool. Fourth are the institutions that draw from one state almost exclusively, and fifth are the state regional colleges and community colleges whose market is a local area that may or may not cross state lines. Finally, there are the increasingly scarce, religiously affiliated institutions where marketing may be national, regional, state, or local but is dominated by considerations of religious affiliation.

Even this division of the industry is arbitrary because great diversity still remains within each sector. An increasingly strong argument might be made that different markets exist for each planned student specialization. However, most students have not developed a specialization by the time of their entry into an undergraduate program, and even if they have, the information system in higher education is so poor that most students are rarely able to consider more than the crudest character of an institution in deciding whether to apply.

There are two important points to be understood in regard to this market structure. First, as noted earlier, the diversity of higher education is itself a marketing device. Second, while there may be only slight competition among institutions for different markets, there will be very strong competition *within* each of these markets. This latter point is often misunderstood by those who see a danger from changes in demand as affecting only the less well known institutions. The pool from which the elite market has traditionally drawn its students is contracting even faster than is the general demographic pool. This relatively greater contraction is due primarily to the lower birthrates found among the highest education and income levels, and secondarily, to the declines in educational quality in primary and secondary education during the last decade. As a result of these forces, an internecine struggle among the elites will be just as vigorously pursued as will be the competition among the marginally legitimate institutions. The difference will be more in the nature of the marketing strategies than in the force of the competition.

For those elite institutions that lose out, the result will be relegation to a lower academic status. For the marginally legitimate schools, the result may be extinction. The institutions who depend on perceived quality of program can do little to affect their basic offerings without jeopardizing the primary market advantage they have. Some may lower the actual quality of their program and depend upon their reputation to carry them for a time. If, as many expect, the economic contraction of higher education lasts well beyond the 1990s, there will be more than enough time for even the weak information system of American higher education to reveal the new condition of these declining institutions.

The marginally legitimate institutions will not have the same constraint on quality adjustments and will depend increasingly on strategies combining lower costs (tuition discounts, nonneed based aid, recognition of prior learning) and reduced intellectual demands. They will succeed only as long as there is a market for academic credentials in isolation from academic content. Higher education, in an attempt to monitor institutions that increasingly deviate from traditional norms of instruction, will face a severe test of will. Unless accrediting agencies are prepared to define and defend a standard of quality, they have no basis for excluding any activity an institution asserts is legitimate.

These traumatic changes throughout the higher education market will produce an alteration in the primary product of higher education—the graduates. If these graduates are significantly different from those of the past, will it still be possible to justify the same forms and amounts of public assistance? To appreciate the issues within this area of concern, it is necessary to understand the nature of social benefits and their relationship to public-support rationales.

The Nature of Social Benefits

In a neoclassical system of public finance, the intervention of government into a market to provide support for a particular good or service may be justified by the belief that the allocative efficiency of the system will be improved. Arguments in support of improving the allocative efficiency of the higher education system through public involvement rely upon the concept of *social benefits*.[1] This concept is really a special case of the "externality" concept that is defined as follows: "An economic externality is said to exist whenever the self-interested action of one individual or group indirectly affects the utility of another individual or group."[2] In less formal terms, the concept implies that certain actions taken will have effects on other parties—for good or ill—but these effects are not the motivation for the original action. For example, a steel mill is not in the business of polluting the air; this is simply an *external* effect of trying to produce steel in the least costly manner. A generalized negative externality of this type is termed a *social cost*.

A social benefit is a generalized positive externality. Innoculation against disease is an example of such an action. Individuals are innoculated because they want to avoid a particular disease themselves, but by this same action they improve the health prospects of other individuals since the innoculated persons are no longer likely to be carriers of the disease. The important ideas in the definition of externalities—either social benefits or costs—are that the original action must be self-interested and the favorable or unfavorable effects produced indirectly from the original action.

The importance of the concept of externalities to public intervention is that without public intervention too much or too little of a particular activity may take place. Societies have controls over pollution to restrict this form of negative externality, and they have subsidies of basic medical innoculation procedures to encourage this social benefit.

Higher education in the United States has long been credited as a source of substantial social benefits. Among the forms of benefits usually cited for higher education, the following are most common:

1. Changes in attitudes and values
2. Improved political leadership and participation
3. The redistribution of income
4. Increased social mobility
5. Increased quantity and quality of research
6. Improved mix of manpower skills
7. Lower unemployment
8. An enhancement of the productivity of physical capital[3]

However, the existence of these benefits is exceedingly uncertain, and their extent and distribution is unknown and probably impossible to quantify. Even if all of the foregoing were resolved and a consensus about benefits were established, that would provide a necessary, but in and of itself, insufficient justification for public intervention. The existence of *marginal* social benefits, i.e., benefits that would be gained only if intervention occurred, would have to be shown to be of sufficient value to justify the taxpayers' sacrifice. Viewed in this perspective, the higher education funding process is left with a single alternative economic explanation: it is a process by which a subset of society is rewarded at the expense of the larger set represented by the taxpayers. Given the social origins of the beneficiaries, one cannot help but question whether the effect of present forms of public intervention are not simultaneously inefficient and inequitable.

Obviously, neither politicians nor the general public yet share this view. There has been growing speculation about public attitudes toward higher education and its cost, but the traditional postsecondary educational systems in the United States remain among the most respected of social institutions. The new era of declining demographics and increased college marketing threatens the public view of (and thereby the public support of) higher education. The nature of these threats and their relationship to the social-benefits concept will be detailed in the following section.

Demographics, Marketing, and Social Benefits

The changing demographic pattern of potential students for higher education will affect the nature and amount of social benefits of higher education in a direct fashion by changing the age pattern of students, and in an indirect fashion by promoting the use of marketing techniques. The altered age pattern could affect social benefits negatively if the older students have an increased interest in exclusively or primarily vocationally oriented curricula. It has long been assumed that the liberal arts orientation of American undergraduate education was the primary source of the changes in attitude and behavior and in improved political leadership that are claimed as social benefits of graduates. If the new clientele of higher education is one for whom these subjects are sacrificed for greater concentration upon vocational courses, then the same claims for social benefits could not be made.

Another way in which the social benefits will be altered is in their duration. Obviously, the older the student, the shorter the period of generation of social benefits by the graduate. It is not by chance that societies have traditionally educated their young; the young have lower opportunity costs and longer periods in which to benefit themselves and society. There are many strong justifications for educational support for the adult population, but the traditional social-benefit argument is probably not one of them.

College marketing activities can threaten the generation of social benefits if the result is to alter the traditional nature of higher education in some basic manner. Again, any increased emphasis on the vocational aspect of higher education will reduce the potential for the generation of social benefits. If interinstitutional competition leads to an increased ease of entry and graduation criteria, the reduced quality of the higher education activities would significantly reduce social-benefits generation. At the extreme one can imagine an institution that has no requirements for graduation other than payment of fees. In a labor market with a strong credential mechanism for entry to many jobs, such an institution may be of benefit to certain types of students. But one can hardly expect the institution to provide an education that will change individuals in some socially beneficial way.

It is useful to view social and student interests as competitive, at least at the margin and probably over a wide range. If the higher educational system or a number of its institutions attempt to maximize student interests — *as perceived by the students at the time* — it is quite probable that both individual student and special interests will be jeopardized. Increasing institutional specialization will reduce the problem of mutual exclusivity among the demands of a diverse student population. However, as institutions specialize, they will face the danger of losing the benefits of tolerance and liberality that their earlier diversity promoted.

The new economic environment for higher education will consist of three conflicting interests: the survival interests of the institution, the financial and educational interests of the student, and the external interests of society. Certain attempts to serve one of these interests are likely to threaten the other two. There is no obvious priority to be assigned between the student and societal interests except that of "right of payment." The larger the proportion of costs borne by students, the greater their right to govern decisions. The greater the educational subsidy, the greater the right of society to impose standards and procedures. The institutional interests are inherently residual since the institution's justification for existence is only in its ability to serve student and/or societal interests.

This conflict of interests is confused by society's delegation to institutions the right and responsibility for control of the higher education product. Academic freedom and institutional autonomy, even of public institutions, were granted in the belief that professional educators best knew how to deal with the interests of both students and society. But the public has become increasingly skeptical of higher education's ability to govern itself, and the last two decades have seen increasing governmental encroachment on the prerogatives of institutions.

A marketing strategy that places a greater emphasis on student interests may alarm those members of the public who are skeptical of students' abilities to make choices about curricular and related issues on long-term rather than short-term bases. Institutions, both public and private, face the danger of making higher education less attractive to taxpayers and voters in an attempt to make it more attractive to students. One alternative, of course, is to increase the proportion of costs paid by students and their families so that societal costs are reduced and thereby a proportion of public taxpayer concern. In addition to the general unpopularity of such a policy, it may be asserted that the public has an interest in higher education even if it is totally privately financed. The government controls many other institutions it does not subsidize, and public control *without* public subsidy is likely to be even more controversial than the present situation.

Before declining into pessimism, it is appropriate to consider whether the college marketing phenomenon is likely to lead to any increase in social benefits. Two major areas of increased benefits would appear to exist. First, the same increased vocationalism that threatens certain attitudinal and behavioral social benefits may actually be supportive of such social benefits as those related to manpower skills, employment rates, material capital productivity, and future tax yields. Second, the changing demographic pattern and the dictates of marketing will mean that greater numbers of students will come from disadvantaged sectors of the population. This pattern of greater social inclusion within higher education should result in increased social mobility for these new members of the student population. This assumes that the new students will receive a quality education; if the institution provides the new student populations with an inferior education, then much of the higher education benefit — to individual and society — will be wasted.

The last is a crucial point. The primary threat of marketing in higher education is not in vocationalization or even in lower admissions standards. The danger is in lowering the standards for graduation with the effect that life opportunities for graduates are not significantly enhanced. Marketing should emphasize special learning assistance for previously disadvantaged populations and possibly even require longer periods to graduation. Unfortunately some students and all too many institutions seem to equate equal educational opportunity or open admissions with reduced intellectual demands and "open graduation." The potential tragedy for higher education lies in the short-sighted nature of this policy.

The present structure of most higher education institutions is well designed to adapt to the vocational needs of students, and with increased tutorial and related support services, to adapt to the needs of adults and to the increased numbers of disadvantaged students. At most colleges and universities students are exposed during the first two years to the type of liberal education most likely to develop the attitudinal and behavioral effects society desires in its citizens. The latter two years of study devoted to specialization can, with increased rigor and improved career counseling, enhance the social benefits related to employment and job productivity. Increased admission of the socially disadvantaged into programs that allow them to graduate with a greater parity to traditional graduates will produce the social benefit inherent in the process of social inclusion.

Marketing thus can be consistent with long-term student and social interests. Concerns about the use of marketing should not be based on inherent conflicts but on conflicts generated by the short-sighted policies of some institutions and the naive demands of certain student groups. Institutions that opt for short-run, survival strategums are likely to find themselves threatened in the long run. The question that remains is which institutions have the courage and commitment in their administration, faculty, and public representatives to look beyond the current need to fill student spaces to the larger responsibility to serve students and society. Those that can do so will bear some transitory costs but eventually should emerge as the strongest institutions as we reach the 1990s and the new century.

Summary and Conclusions

The discussion here concerning marketing and social benefits may be summarized as follows:

- The use of marketing is not a new development in higher education, but the emphasis on short-term student concerns is both new and dangerous in its emphasis.
- Marketing in higher education takes place not within a single student market but in a complex of markets. Within which market a college will compete for students is determined by institutional characteristics such as public or private control, perceived quality, geographic area of competition, size, costs, and a variety of other factors influencing student choice.
- Public support of higher education is rationally justified primarily through the production of social benefits that would not be produced in the absence of subsidization.
- The various forms of social benefits attributed to higher education are debatable as to their existence, their amount, and their incidence.
- Whether or not marginal social benefits actually exist in amounts adequate to justify present levels of subsidization, the public support for higher education is maintained in large part because of public *belief* in the existence of social benefits.
- The current demographic determinants of demand for higher education and the increased use of marketing techniques pose both threats and opportunities for the production of social benefits.
- While, in the short term, institutional, student, and social interests may appear to conflict, the long-run interests of each would seem to demand a maintenance of educational quality.

Much of the discussion in this paper is necessarily based upon conjecture rather than evidence. But here, as in most public policy areas, logical and historical patterns of behavior are our best guides. The inertia of social institutions is such that once embarked upon a generalized strategy of reduced demand and rigor, higher education would be difficult to reclaim. As this paper has attempted to emphasize, it is not marketing, demographics, or even a lack of ethics that poses the greatest threat to public interests in higher education. It is the inability of individuals and institutions to look beyond the immediate need for full enrollments to the important maintenance of quality education.

References

1. For a detailed discussion of the social-benefit controversy the reader is referred to D. M. Windham, "The Public Responsibility for Higher Education: Policy Issues and Research Directions," in *Subsidies to Higher Education*, H. Tuckman and E. Whalen, editors. New York: Praeger Press, forthcoming.

2. D. M. Windham, *Planning Higher Education: Alternatives in Theory, Research, and Policy*. Paris: International Institute of Educational Planning, 1978, p. 74.

3. A discussion of these benefit forms and their relevance to public involvement may be found in D. W. Windham, "Social Benefits and the Subsidization of Higher Education: A Critique," *Higher Education*, Vol. 5, 1976, pp. 237-252.

Marketing and the Future of Institutions

by Barbara S. Uehling

Marketing to the average individual suggests images of piles of fresh vegetables hawked by bandanna-covered peddlers, a salesperson knocking at the door, individuals in plaid suits and striped ties carrying cases onto airplanes, or a department of college graduates manning computers and conducting analyses of the activities of a large corporation. None of these seems to have much to do with higher education. Or does it? Do we have a product that is being offered to individuals for a price, that they can purchase or reject? Obviously we do, and we have been involved in marketing for some time, although with varying degrees of recognition of what we are doing. Some institutional presentations seem directed, while in others the activity is haphazard. In fact, the marketing approaches of institutions are not unlike a classification of marketing managers I recently read.

"There are those who make things happen.
There are those who think they make things happen.
There are those who watch things happen.
There are those who wonder what happened.
There are those who did not know anything happened."[1]

The marketing activity of many educational institutions is reflected in the last statement. Marketing has occurred, but there is no realization that something actually has happened!

In recent years institutions of higher education have begun to turn to marketing for a number of reasons. These undoubtedly include declining enrollments, projections of still further declines in the 18- to 21-year-old population, budget concerns, competition among institutions, and probably more than anything else, a need to maintain what we have already created regardless of its present or future value. As a result of these concerns, we have looked to business and industry where marketing is the approved mode of operation.

The application of marketing techniques in higher education has raised some important questions. Are we falsifying? Are we distorting the facts in our marketing activities? Are we being unethical when we become very blatant in our approach to recruitment of students? I read recently of a state higher education institution that had planned to release 103 balloons with scholarship offers, until someone pointed out that perhaps the approach was inappropriate. A prestigious southern institution recently paid for a supplement in the *New York Times*. We have not yet, to the best of my knowledge, offered toasters or ovens, as is done in banking, but we may not be very far from it. Are we distorting the purpose of higher education by boldly displaying our wares, or are we perhaps trying to meet the needs of inappropriate customers? For example, is that course in scuba diving, which has just attracted an increased enrollment, really an appropriate activity for the enterprise of higher education?

My topic is to discuss the concept of marketing as it applies to the future of higher education, particularly future enrollments. I am going to be doing this from the perspective of a single institution because of my present status as an institutional head. I can also rationalize this approach by remembering that the future of higher education will be the result of the sum of activities of all institutions. How well each institution markets and how responsibly will determine the net result. I shall start with a definition of marketing that is helpful to my thinking. Philip Kotler, a recognized authority on marketing, has said: "The core concern of marketing is that of producing desired responses in free individuals by the judicious creation and offering of values. The marketer is attempting to get value from the market through offering value to it."[2]

There are several points in this definition that are particularly meaningful and worthy of further reflection. First, in marketing we are, in fact, offering something to individuals who have a choice; we are not forcing anything on them. The fact that they have a choice is important to the way in which we approach them. Second, we should be oriented to the needs of those individuals who have that choice. Third, by these activities, we can judiciously create value. The creation of value is something perfectly appropriate to higher education, and indeed, quite attractive to the enterprise because we believe in the intrinsic worth of our product and want to convince others of its value. Finally, in offering value, we also can derive value from the market. In other words, we gain. While the gain is not as obvious as it is in an industry or business organized for profit, we nevertheless gain. We profit by receiving support to carry on the activity that we value, and we gain psychologically because we are making an important contribution to our society.

Thus, if we look at marketing as an activity that meets needs, creates worth, and derives value, it is highly appropriate for higher education. Clearly, we have been involved in these activities for a long time.

The introduction of marketing as a new concept is advantageous because it facilitates the asking of questions not readily apparent otherwise. These questions point to the future and support possible change. For example, whose needs are to be met? How are those needs presently being met? What value should be added by higher education? What process can an educational institution employ to add value? Who has the responsibility for initiating and determining the process?

This paper will offer a decision model for marketing that is in actuality a plan for the future. If we in higher education are going to continue to create value, we must initially meet the needs of our clientele as they exist. In designing and executing that plan, an-

Figure 1. Decision Model for Marketing

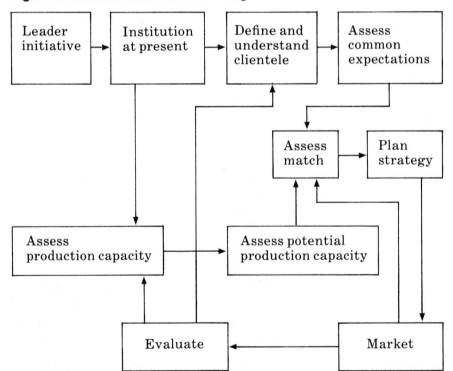

swers to the above questions will be found. A flow diagram offered at the outset should be helpful to understanding the remainder of the paper. Figure 1 depicts a series of decision points that can culminate in an institutional marketing plan.

Leader Initiative

The initiative to engage in a plan for improved marketing must be at the instigation of an institutional head. Any real hope of success with an effort to build a model, which may change institutional focus and presentation of that focus, lies in the active engagement of the task by the institutional head. Responsibilities for specific components, of course, may and probably will be designated. However, the initiation of a marketing perspective and maintenance of that perspective by the leader is essential.

In addition to simply initiating and maintaining a perspective, the head of the institution will need to establish a rational framework for the generation and delivery of services in the institution. He or she will need to establish an administrative framework that makes planning possible and rewarding, and to create in the institution a sense of fairness, purpose, and optimism. And, finally, the leader will be responsible for how well this decision model works, for its implementation, and for its evaluation and subsequent modification.

Institution at Present

The first step in executing a marketing plan is to identify the characteristics of the institution at the outset. An understanding of its history can in some circumstances provide a useful perspective but most often is unnecessary. Rather, the focus should be on characteristics such as number and types of programs, number and qualifications of faculty, financial health, trends in enrollment, trends in support, services provided, size and condition of physical plant, and attitudes of faculty and staff. Other information will be needed and is worthy of more extensive discussion. This will follow in the next two steps, defining and understanding clientele and assessing production capacity.

Define and Understand Clientele

Looking again at the flow chart, the next upper box represents the need to define and understand the clientele of an institution. The ability to define the clientele differs from institution to institution.

For some, the constraints of legislative definition, the heritage of selective admissions practices, or the biases of the governing board may aid in the active definition of student clientele. In other instances, considerable latitude exists. But regardless of how much latitude exists in the definition and selection of clientele, the characteristics of the clientele groups can at least be understood.

The most obvious clientele group, and almost the exclusive target of marketing approaches, is students. The model approach to students as clientele has often been a passive acceptance of those who arrive on our doorsteps under routine programs. Little initiative in trying to change that clientele or to attract more students with particular characteristics has occurred. Our attempts to understand potential and realized students have varied greatly.

Often information is collected about entrance scores, home address, grade-point average in high school, and finally, age and sex. But we know very little about students' backgrounds, the socioeconomic level of the parents, the kinds of values students were taught, employment demands and experience, or expectations of a college education. Is the most important expectation a job; is it a growing sense of personal identity; is it to have fun, to be identified with a prestigious enterprise; or is it a more vague and more abstract long-range goal about personal growth and fulfillment?

There are other important clientele groups for whom a marketing approach is needed. Parents comprise such a group. The importance of parents as clientele is not consistent across institutions because of age differences among students, residential status, and differing dependency patterns of students upon parents. But in some institutions the parents may be even more important than the students. As a rule, the expectations of parents about an institution probably do not differ much from students in kind, only in priority. Parents are more likely to be interested in safety, psychological climate, and wholesomeness of the social environment than are students. Parents may also place a higher priority on the quality of the academic programs.

Alumni, donors, and taxpayers also comprise important clientele groups, and all have expectations about higher education. Those expectations may include football successes, recognition of personal or present accomplishments, or interest in the development of specific academic programs with which selected alumni, donors, or taxpayers happen to be affiliated. As important, they may have more generalized expectations about what should happen in our society as a result of higher education. Whatever they may be, these are real expectations that influence the behavior of these groups toward higher education and an institution.

A final clientele group that deserves mention are employers. Employers may also be members of another clientele, but as employers they are concerned primarily with the development of a special human resource, that is, potential employees with particular sets of skills and abilities. More and more employers are interested in growth potential as well as the operational skills evident in graduates the day the person is hired.

In view of the number of clientele groups, it is tempting to stress the variety of their expectations and to take the posture that such diverse needs cannot be met. So why try? However, if we examine these factors more closely, there are those that are common to all clientele groups of any institution. For example, all may expect employment, the development of leadership, a responsible citizenry, and personal individual fulfillment. Institutions can attempt to accommodate these common expectations in programmatic directions and in the learning experiences provided. The taxpayer, the alumnus, and the employer may also have a common concern, an expectation that the institution provide basic research that will benefit both society and the corporate world. On the other hand, some students, taxpayers, and employers may expect continuing education, extension, or service-oriented offerings to adults. A very important common expectation, the development of human potential, is even more difficult to address because of the ambiguity of definition of the goal.

The attempts to determine common needs and accommodate them can vary in their formality. Abstract models are available to assist in determining overlapping preferences or common expectations. However, a sufficient initial determination can be made by less formal analyses based on information from interviews or survey instruments. Whatever our technique, the systematic sampling of all clientele groups will prevent us from focusing on a few adamant, vocal individuals. It is much too easy in administration to attend to the expectations of the few who use a telephone or mail barrage. An approach that samples clientele will be far more meaningful to the building of a sound marketing approach.

Most important, from this process will come a knowledge about what clientele value in higher education and what should be valued that is not presently valued — what value must be created. For example, a merchant might find that brightly colored plastic beads are the valued adornment of a particular group of people when that merchant has pearls to sell. The value of pearls should be obvious, but the merchant has first to recognize that the value is not obvious and then begin a program to create value, such as pointing out that pearls are more enduring than plastic beads, or that they are more scarce and therefore to be more valued. A program in astrology may have wide appeal, but the responsibility of a university is to show that real understanding of behavior is generated only by research and is gained only by those with access to research methodology. Some are concerned that we in higher education will give up pearls and offer the equivalent of plastic beads. That, of course, is not the appropriate marketing approach for higher education.

Assess Production Capacity

Referring again to the flow chart, the assessment of the production capacity can be conducted simultaneously with that of the investigation of clientele needs. Marketing applied to higher education may seem foreign but can be helpful in gaining new insights into our activities. In this framework we can analyze the following factors: producers, programs, price, physical facilities, market shares, and image.

Producers. The faculty of any institution are the primary producers of education, supplemented by the support staff. The qualifications, abilities, number, and attitudes of both faculty and staff are the most basic elements of the process for producing educational services.

Faculty are also of critical importance because they are the principal, if not sole, determiners of curriculum and program development. Historically, they have created programs with little reference to clientele groups, probably because of no incentives to do otherwise, but that practice has led in some instances to decreasing attractiveness or relevance to these groups. Another problem is that the faculty producers have often functioned without an overall rationale or framework, which should be provided by the institutional leadership. Seldom are curricular proposals tested against well-defined principles for institutional decision making. As a result, many catalogs list aggregations of courses representing the specific training and biases of the faculty program definers.

A further reason for the importance of faculty is their interaction with students. This is the fundamental ingredient of the learning experience.

Considering all the above points, it is not surprising to identify faculty as the basic element of production, and to recognize that any change in production must mean a change in faculty or in the organization and incentive structure for the faculty.

Program. It is also necessary to look at program offerings as an essential component of production. Their diversity, level, and quality are apparent targets for assessment. Viewing program characteristics from a marketing approach may be difficult because such assessments are typically done without reference to clientele needs and perceptions. Assessment criteria have been primarily those generated by producers rather than consumers. Peer estimates used in evaluation of faculty have sometimes taken precedence over consumer criteria such as attractiveness to students, communicability, relevance to perceptions based on background, and employer views of programs. Research may or may not be judged by expectations of clientele groups, but societal needs are an important consideration.

Price. Price is a factor that has not been studied as carefully by public institutions as by private ones. Whether public or private (but nonproprietary), the treatment of price is necessarily different from that of business since other subsidies of education partially support the costs of providing the service marketed. We expect understanding by clientele that we are not-for-profit organizations and are offering our product at no profit. But if we reduce price to the direct consumer, other things being equal, the price to the indirect consumer will need to increase.

Serious analyses of the production process must look carefully at price to determine if it should change or to determine if the mix of support from student fees, state, federal, and donor support should change. What other mixes are possible, likely, or most compatible with clientele groups?

Physical facilities. The physical conditions in which learning and living occur certainly contribute to the production capacity of an institution. A frequent emphasis on condition and type of equipment is only a part of the concern. It is easy to recognize that computers, modern laboratory equipment, and instructional media are essential parts of a learning environment. Often unrecognized as important are the physical arrangements for study, eating, leisure, student-faculty interactions, and an environment reflective of important social realities. How much is human learning enhanced by an appropriate physical environment, and how much is it impeded by the extra energy required to cope with a less than desirable one?

Market share. A production measure that business has usefully employed is market share. An institution will find it valuable in assessing its existing production pattern and production trends to know what proportion of the students in its region among peer institutions attend that institution. Or it will be useful to know what proportion of the research dollars given in particular programs come to that institution, or what proportion of all donor dollars given to institutions in a particular region, size, and type come to the institution in question. Finally, it is valuable to know what percentage of all graduates hired in an area are graduates of that institution. This knowledge can lead to an understanding of why these market shares are held.

Image. The image held by clientele groups is still another way in which to assess the provision of educational services. What is the perception of the institution? Is it viewed as comprehensive, individualistic, a good place for professional training, elitist, responsive, nontraditional, aloof, accessible, social? Is it people oriented? Is it well managed? If the external image of an institution is inconsistent with what is intended, the production of educational services may be inefficient. On the other hand, production could be adequate but marketing inadequate or inaccurate.

Assess Potential for Change

It is highly unlikely that in the present type of analysis the perfect institutional approach will be found. Almost certainly, change will be needed, so the most efficient way to proceed is to identify such potentials while analyzing the present state. In identifying the potential there should not be an attempt to presume the outcome of the analysis. However, the factors that will result in resistance to change and those that will facilitate change can be identified. There are many forces acting against change in the academic world — both real and imagined. Tenure, financial trends, and tradition all can mitigate against change. Persistence in following past patterns will be the most likely course of action in the face of no other plan. However, the influx of new ideas, the appeal to pride, and even the need to escape boredom can all represent forces for change.

There will be areas in which change can be more easily accomplished than others. Measures such as faculty turnover rates, retirement rates, and history of curricular changes should all be routinely collected data and will give clues to ready conditions for change. But changes may need to be created in new ways. Perhaps small grants for curriculum changes can be offered, or budgetary rewards for making needed adjustments.

In assessing potential change other aspects of production capacity identified in the previous section also must be analyzed. What can be accomplished in the physical environment? What new directions in research are probable? Possible? How firmly is the legislature or board committed to particular entrance requirements or to particular definitions of mission? How strongly are present institutional images held?

Assess Match

Assessing whether current production capacities fit clientele needs is somewhat like the task of a marriage broker in deciding if an already arranged match is a good fit. There may be a tendency to select only those attributes for comparison in which it appears that all is bliss. But critical honesty is a necessity if any rectification of past problems is to be achieved or even if understanding of present success is to be built upon.

Although focusing on particular elements of the institution that are already matching clientele needs could create a feeling of security, looking at other institutional components might show clientele needs are not being met. The Business School may be turning out employable graduates, but the College of Arts and Science has taken pride in remaining heavily committed to traditional programs with little responsiveness to employment needs of students. The result is an uneven institutional meeting of clientele needs. Two or three departments may excel in research dollars attracted, yet the great majority are doing little in this area. The student life programs may stress mutual responsibilities, while a sense of community is never discussed in the classroom nor demonstrated in actions of personnel. Matching the clientele needs should occur for all relevant segments, not just a visible few.

Plan Strategy

It is interesting that we in education have recently adopted a military term, strategy, as the appropriate word to describe our schemes for the future. However described, a plan should be developed that is forward looking and will guide future decisions and describe conditions for initiating decisions. It will probably be helpful to divide the task into short- and long-range strategies.

Some very quick and inexpensive things, almost cosmetic in nature, could be done to meet short-term and highly visible goals. On the other hand, if we are responsible as educators for creating value, we shall need long-range strategies that will help shape our clientele needs at the same time we are adapting ourselves. Strategy, as implied by the plan, should try to create as great a match as possible in the short run, but should also pose a longer time frame in which the creation of value and subsequent perceptions of clientele may shift. Consider some examples. In the short term, students may want to develop personally and socially even more than to acquire disciplinary skills. Parents are generally not opposed to these personal and social goals but in addition desire safety of the environment, both psychological and physical. The taxpayer or donor is also not opposed to those initial goals of students, although these goals may not be placed in as high a priority. However, they also desire that these personal-development activities occur in a wholesome environment. The need for personal and social development of students, which is common to all groups, could likely be met better than at present with relatively little cost. It might be accomplished by arranging small noncredit seminars, and encouraging faculty advisers to talk with students about their feelings, attitudes, and development. Faculty-student discussions on a variety of topics might be scheduled outside the classroom. Faculty involvement has the additional benefit of familiarizing the producers with the wide range of clientele needs. Faculty who are almost always eager to do a good job may make accommodations to reach students more effectively without additional stimulation. The long-term strategy of all their efforts would be to help students through personal development toward interest in knowledge, which in turn assists them to further growth.

Another example of a common need is employment. Students, parents, employers, and taxpayers all want employment to be a result of higher education. To meet this need in the short term, an improved placement service might be developed, internship or work-study programs established, obvious or easy modifications of courses or curriculum undertaken, or employers asked to serve in advisory groups. As a long-term strategy, evaluations would need to be conducted and greater programmatic changes might be initiated. At the same time, in an effort to create value, all clientele groups, but particularly employers, can be engaged in participating experiences with faculty and students. In that way an understanding can be developed of the contributions of a liberal arts curriculum that teaches problem definition and solution, and knowledge of how others have met and answered challenges in the past, and that focuses on positive attitudes and self-confidence.

Whether the strategy is short or long term, those who will be responsible for its implementation must be involved in its formation. That means that administrators cannot plan for faculty, nor faculty for administrators. Both will be involved in implementation, and both must be involved in the planning of strategy. No matter how good the strategy, if its development occurs in secret or if the results are imposed rather than adopted, it will not result in success. It should also be made clear that while strategy planning is occurring, the institution will change as will its external environment. The strategy will need to be reviewed as these shifts occur. Any resulting alterations will also need to involve participation by those responsible for implementation.

Market

The result of successful strategy planning should be a proposed set of operational steps. The overall approach can be described by *what* should be marketed, *who* is responsible, and *how* it is to be done.

What? It should be a simple task following strategy planning to characterize the institution and its programs in general easily understood descriptions. These should be designed to appeal to clientele, not producers. For example, the institutional profile might be characterized as comprehensive, graduate and undergraduate, residential, traditional, historical. Or it might be small, personal, flexible, individualistic, appealing to moderate-ability students. The general description will, of course, need to be accompanied by some specific statements about aspects of special concern to particular market segments. These specific descriptions will refer to student life, faculty, and physical characteristics of the campus. The marketing descriptions used for different clientele may vary somewhat in content, but should not be inconsistent. For example, the profile targeted for students might emphasize the graduate-training focus, while for taxpayers and donors, research productivity. But both are aspects of the same program. Above all, the institutional identity needs to remain paramount and to be well articulated.

Who? Everyone identified with an institution can be thought of as carrying a billboard advertising some characteristic or set of characteristics typical of the institution. In short, everyone is involved in marketing: students, faculty, administrators, staff, alumni. The message to be marketed should be so clearly understood and so widespread in its dissemination that all representatives are at ease in transmitting it.

How? Creativity, good judgment, and integrity should be the primary determinants in marketing. Those who are chiefly responsible for disseminating information concerning the purpose and identity of the institution should plan to direct their activities in a way that is consistent with those purposes and priorities. If "personalness" is a major goal of the institution, the entire staff should be individually involved and alert to the specific strategies employed to create an environment of people-orientation as well as to instances when that orientation is manifested. If research is the goal and therefore an important external message, the collections of information about research, its benefit to the state, and long-term benefits to society become important directions for the public-information effort. An activity analysis of the information office in terms of institutional goals and priorities can be valuable.

Evaluate

Once all these steps are in motion, it might seem that efforts can be relaxed and all that is needed is to wait for the results. Not yet! Even at the outset of a plan, evaluation must be initiated. Decisions must be made in advance about what analytical measures will be used and who has the responsibility for conducting the evaluation. A time frame must also be established, or some signals devised that will suggest things are not working and an inventory is needed.

After evaluation, other modifications in the strategy will likely be needed. It is best if a continuing mechanism to create and accommodate change is established. In how many institutions has a plan been devised, admired, even implemented, without an understanding of the need for an evaluation mechanism or for subsequent alterations. It is equally important to decide in advance who has the responsibility for evaluation and for modification.

Recommendations

It seems appropriate to offer some specific recommendations that may be used by an institution to implement a future marketing strategy. Seven general principles and examples of some specific targets within the general principles are given below.

1. The definition and solicitation of clientele should be an active process. Even existing restraints that limit clientele groups can be appropriate targets for change.

Targets:

- Present clientele characteristics
- Market segmentation
- Recruiting locations, personnel, and approaches
- Entrance requirements
- Alumni–potential-student contacts
- Media presentations

2. The assessment of production should be inclusive. Often the definition of productivity or the production potential is unduly narrow and exclusive of important elements of production such as institutional services, staff morale, and community attitudes.

Targets:

- Number and types of programs
- Qualifications, number, and program distribution of faculty
- Fiscal resources
- Physical plant resources
- Staff numbers and qualifications
- Budget allocations[3]
- Market-share indices

3. Planned change and likely unplanned change both need to be considered in assessing the common expectations, the production potential, and the future match. Not only do we need to plan desired changes, but we need to look at trends over which we have no control and adjust the match as much as possible.

Targets:

- Clientele needs and perceptions
- Financing trends
- Extraordinary budget demands
- Faculty flexibility
- Employment trends
- Societal demands
- National attitudes and policy regarding education

4. In planning strategy, information, participation by those who must implement, construction of incentives, and implementation capability are all needed.

Targets:
- Information systems
- Governance mechanisms
- Personnel policies
- Incentive systems
- Administrative organization
- Operational analysis of subunits

5. Marketing is a total institutional commitment.

Targets:
- Program definition
- Need accommodation
- Value creation
- Internal and external communication
- Task assignment to individuals and units
- Budget adjustments

6. Evaluation should be a continuous activity, with adjustment mechanisms built in. Small adjustments are preferable to major modifications.

Targets:
- Clientele
- Programs
- Faculty and staff
- Physical facilities
- Budget
- Image
- Scheduling and location

7. No matter what techniques are used or how sophisticated or unsophisticated the system, the best marketing that can possibly be done by an institution is to have a good quality product that does, in fact, meet the needs of its clientele groups, while it is working to create value for that product in those groups. If these conditions exist, the enterprise should succeed.

References

1. John Naylor and Alan Wood, *Practical Marketing Audits: A Guide to Increased Profitability.* New York: John Wiley and Sons, 1978, p. 10.

2. Philip Kotler, "The Generic Concept of Marketing," *Journal of Marketing*, Vol. 36, April 1972, p. 50.
3. An interesting exercise would be the analysis of budget expenditures by identified clientele need.

Marketing Higher Education: A Reappraisal

by Larry H. Litten

Marketing has long been part of the true story of American colleges and universities—only the terminology has changed (and some of the techniques refined) to promote the expedient. Ever since Harvard began granting degrees befóre it was legally chartered and Yale followed at some distance to provide a less liberal brand of education, American colleges and universities have sought to provide a distinctive set of educational services to a particular clientele. The early nineteenth century saw a proliferation of colleges to cater to sectarian interests, then colleges emerged to serve women exclusively, and in the late nineteenth century a rash of institutions developed to serve various farm and labor interests. Throughout our history, our academic institutions have been responding to, as well as contributing to, the continual change that has marked American society and culture. Often their marketing activities have even helped to create an awareness of the need for particular kinds of higher education.[1] Laurence Veysey has recounted how some of these efforts have been reflected in the recruitment and admissions activities of colleges (see pages 5-22).*

Current expediencies arise from the desire of colleges to remain viable in view of the reduced demand anticipated from the shrinkages of age groups they have traditionally served. Compounding this concern are the financial pressures that are particularly severe in inflationary times for labor-intensive institutions. Higher education has been captured by a preoccupation that is analogous to a concern for growth: a desire to minimize the effects of a general demographic decline on each institution. Colleges and universities, therefore, have taken a strong interest in the concepts, principles, and techniques of marketing as developed and applied in business — a sphere in which growth and relations with the market have been of much more central concern than in higher education. The push from within higher education to exploit the marketing techniques of business converged with a heightened drive within marketing to bring its principles and techniques to the service of a variety of nonbusiness areas.[2]

---

* Page numbers in parentheses in this chapter refer to other articles in the present volume.

A great deal has been written about marketing in higher education since the first College Board colloquium on the subject.[3] The adoption of formal marketing concepts and techniques by colleges and universities has both advocates and opponents. It has become apparent, however, that marketing, as it has been promoted, will not be the salvation of higher education; as it has been attacked, it is not the rapacious monster so often caricatured. A basic premise of this paper is that market research and marketing can be useful to higher education – if done sensibly. Furthermore, I believe the general practice of marketing might be enriched if the marketing issues of higher education are successfully resolved.

The Potentials and Pitfalls of Current Marketing Theory and Practice

The Cases For and Against Marketing

Friends of marketing are found both inside and outside academia, although within higher education it is primarily institutional administrators who have advocated or defended the use of formal marketing practices. Market researchers in higher education have already made substantial contributions to our understanding of the market for higher education. Proponents of marketing practices have argued persuasively that through effective use of the marketing mix (program development, pricing policy, promotional practices, and provision of educational offerings), a college can serve students better, increase its attractiveness, and thereby increase demand for its services.[4] Although less attention has been given to the benefits that marketing can bring to the system of higher education, it is claimed that increased institutional diversity, educational efficiency and effectiveness, and an overall expansion of useful services could result from properly conceived and implemented marketing activities.[5]

There is no question that colleges operate in markets with a number of suppliers competing to provide services to a multitude of publics and individuals who need or desire them. Kotler and Levy's classic observation stands: "The choice facing those who manage nonbusiness organizations is not whether to market or not market, for no organization can avoid marketing. The choice is whether to do it well or poorly, and on this necessity the case for organizational marketing is basically founded.[6]

Arguments against marketing in higher education have come

primarily from academicians (pages 92-120), but journalists have recently joined the fray.[7] There is no question but that the powerful tools of marketing can be misused and that some undesirable practices have developed.

As the debate continues, two facts have become apparent:

▪ Academicians are often embarrassingly ignorant of the scope and complexities of marketing as it is discussed by marketers. The problem is not restricted to faculty who sequester themselves behind ivy-covered walls; even some who write on the subject of marketing exhibit poor comprehension of the phenomenon they are treating.

▪ For the most part, marketers are appallingly unaware of the nature of higher education and its responsibilities, or in their zeal they choose to ignore these realities. Their behavior is often more congruent with the negative images held of them by academicians than with the principles of their discipline.

As a result of this situation, the advocacy of marketing is frequently misdirected by being based on misperceptions and false assumptions about higher education; opposition to marketing misses some of the major problems while tilting with some marginal or specious issues.

I doubt that these failings will seriously affect the essential nature of the academy. There are sufficient institutional safeguards in the system to prevent that from happening. The greater problem is that much effort will be wasted promoting misguided schemes, that misperceptions by the public will be perpetuated and compounded, and that there may be a public reaction against some of the peripheral excesses perpetrated in the name of academic marketing. The real contributions that marketing and market research could make to higher education may indeed be sacrificed as they are mispromoted and misresisted.

The Marketing Myopia of the Academician

It is all too common to find academic personnel nurturing the belief that marketing is simply promotional activities. Little recognition is given to the fact that the courses offered, the quality of faculty, entrance and graduation requirements, tuition levels and financing arrangements, extracurricular activities, residential arrangements, off-campus programs, and athletic policy are all marketing phenomena. They affect what benefits a college offers, how attractive it is, with what other institutions it competes, and thus how it relates to its market. Indeed, Harvard is not above marketing, as is often implied—it is simply one of the most successful marketers in American academic history.

Even the academicians' attacks on *promotion* fail to recognize the important informational components of such activities. As John Hoy pointed out, the effective communication of information about a college is a legitimate and important activity. It is also a difficult challenge that will not be performed well without considerable attention and effort (see pages 99-102). Some critics have focused specifically on the persuasive aspect of promotion.[8] Their complaints sometimes relate to real promotional abuses, but their blanket condemnations overlook some important considerations as well. Persuasion, per se, is not illegitimate—we teach this very art in our English and speech courses. Motivation is hardly foreign to higher education—no good teacher ignores the need to motivate students. The integrity of higher education will not be compromised by scrupulous promotional activities that involve the provision of information in an appealing and persuasive manner. To seek to be attractive is not an unworthy objective for a college when coupled with other principles of honesty and honor.

There is often an assumption, sometimes implicit, that competitive marketing in higher education will compromise quality (see pages 108-120). For reasons explored in greater detail below, that risk certainly exists. Nevertheless, quality is itself a major marketing tool, and the production and distribution of quality merchandise and services have strong traditions in business. There are substantial segments of the higher education system in which competition is based largely on efforts to provide ever-enhanced educational quality. To suggest that either competition or marketing will *necessarily* dilute quality is to misunderstand the place of quality in marketing and to tender a mean general indictment of the American population—particularly those adults who have already received a quality education and who advise many prospective student consumers.

Critics of marketing have also suggested that it ignores individuals in favor of groups (see pages 94-95). On the contrary, customized services also have a strong tradition in marketing. Marketing's frequent attention to groups is not intrinsic; it is a function of the basic fact that any individualized service is very expensive. Furthermore, group activities and common educational experiences have as strong a philosophical justification in education as does individualized activity; both are necessary.

Finally, critics of marketing in higher education often fail to make appropriate distinctions between sectors of the higher education system. Criticism that may be justified regarding marketing directed to recent high school graduates does not necessarily apply to marketing directed toward mature adult learners.

The Myopic Marketing of the Marketers

Marketers have failed to present a good, basic definition of marketing, and in their efforts to broaden their sphere of activities, their definitions sometimes embrace the totality of human activity.[9] Central to much marketing activity, however, is the *marketing concept* (see page 45) and the idea of a *responsive organization* — "one that accepts its customers as members and abides by their will in marketing decisions."[10]

Few marketers show the sensibilities to the limited applicability of the marketing concept to higher education that is evidenced by Christopher Lovelock and Michael Rothschild (pages 31-69) or William Ihlanfeldt (pages 70-91).[11] The following remarks are an elaboration of their observations and address the level of misunderstanding of higher education more generally manifested by marketers.

Failures of Understanding or Appreciation. To date, marketers have not appreciated fully the nature of the "products and services" of higher education, the "consumers" of higher education, the "firms," nor the "market."

The Product. Higher education embraces a vast array of products and services, including some of the most complex and advanced "products" in our society. Marketers have tended to focus primarily on the provision of educational services to students, and most often on instructional programs. Furthermore, since the demographic decline is the source of much of the interest in marketing, a college's *potential* students have been the principal focus of marketing attention. Yet it is important to recognize that not only is instruction but a part of the services rendered to students, but also service to students is only one of the several functions of higher education. As Douglas Windham has discussed (see pages 124-126), public subsidies for both institutions and students are justified on the basis of benefits to the public beyond the private benefits of student consumers.

Among the several services provided students in addition to instruction are certification of knowledge and skills possessed; socialization to the norms and standards of intellectual activity; an environment for psychological maturation; a setting and means for socialization to adult roles; and opportunities for physical development, for socializing and entertainment, and in some colleges, for daily sustenance and for religious development.

The socializing functions of colleges present a particularly difficult set of problems to the marketer following the marketing concept of being responsive to the consumer. Although often limited in the degree to which it is realized, the existence of a community of scholars and their apprentices who adhere to a particular ethos is still an important aspect of the academic ideal. Though contemporary realization of this ideal is limited, to surrender it would be to forfeit even hope of such communities. It is difficult to envision a responsive institution exemplifying the ideals that socialize young people to the highest norms of intellectual life; responsive organizations, as typically discussed by marketers, are more likely *to conform* to the norms and expressed desires of consumers.

There are products and services of higher education that are not directly included in the instruction of students but relate to those processes in critical ways. Universities and colleges are expected to preserve knowledge and cultural and intellectual traditions, and to discover and transmit the wisdom of the past. Likewise, the creation and dissemination of new knowledge are fundamental functions of higher education. These pursuits must follow the dictates and canons of intellectual inquiry, even though they may lead into areas or arrive at conclusions that are unfamiliar or even unpopular with the public. Indeed, higher education has developed a hardwon institution to facilitate adherance to intellectual norms — tenure of faculty members. It is intended to function essentially as a buffer *against* direct pressures from the market. Misguided attempts to be responsive could reduce the power of this device and compromise the essential intellectual functions in our society that it was designed to protect and advance.

Important interdependencies exist between the several products and services of higher education. The nature and quality of scholarship affects the nature and quality of teaching and vice versa. These interdependencies were duly recognized after much debate in an earlier movement to adapt business practices in cost accounting and financial control to higher education. The phenomena were referred to as joint products — e.g., funds spent on research contribute to the vigor of teaching, and research benefits from the criticism it receives in the classroom. Marketers have generally overlooked the complexities of joint-production processes in their prescriptions for higher education.

One area where marketing often violates a fundamental academic precept is the growing tendency to treat institutional market research as proprietary, completely contrary to the norm of open inquiry. It is a dangerous infection of the academic system, particularly when the information gained relates to general human values and behavior and not just the public's perceptions of a particular institution or set of institutions.

The judgment of importance and quality in intellectual products and services is necessarily a matter of professional consensus.[12] Although educational services can be offered at various levels of sophistication to students with various capacities for judging them, the faculty play an essential role in the determination of educational products. Those persons who know an intellectual or professional field in its broadest and deepest extensions have both the authority and responsibility to make judgments on behalf of those with more limited perspective. This is not to say that students do not have a role to play in evaluating the efficacy of instruction, but even then appropriate perspective is often lacking for consumers who have just "consumed." A serious concern in marketing higher education is not consumer dissatisfaction, but rather unwarranted satisfaction.

Higher education is also responsible for contributing to the formation of highly skilled manpower for our economy. Not only is the content of training for such occupational roles better known by the professional educator than most students, a student with imperfect information is often in a poor position to know what the labor market rewards or even what all the occupational options are. Higher education must be responsive, to a certain extent, to the labor market for highly skilled manpower and has the responsibilities of educating naive consumers regarding their options and helping to motivate students toward areas of national need. In this particular aspect of academic marketing, combinations of responsiveness and promotion are in order, with primary responsiveness not to the traditional consumer, but to the eventual consumers (employers) of the immediate consumers' (students') services.

The Consumers. For several reasons marketers have focused their attention on the student consumer in higher education, to the exclusion of other consumers. Students can answer market research questionnaires; the needs of the economy, the political system, and the society at large cannot be as easily ascertained. Furthermore, aspects of the system of higher education favor traditional, individual consumer-oriented marketing approaches. It is largely a student-consumer driven system, with enrollment-based financing in both the public and independent sectors. However, when too much emphasis is placed on the student as the decision maker and as the bearer of specific demands or expectations to drive the "responsive" collegiate organization, there is the risk of overlooking the other important functions, services, and beneficiaries of higher education.

Students vary in their sophistication, maturity, and desires. The most problematic set of consumers for the responsive marketer is the traditional prospective student – the high school senior. Often these students are not reliable sources of information about important aspects of the academic marketing mix, especially the curriculum (the instructional "product" or service). A young person graduating from high school frequently knows only vaguely what educational benefits he or she wants and only a little about what he or she needs.[13] Much of the capacity for judging and criticizing higher education can only come as a result of the knowledge and skills that are developed through participation in its programs. Furthermore, a quality collegiate education ought to be a powerful source of personal change and development; unimagined perspectives on one's self, one's circumstances, and one's society ought to emerge from such experiences. In addition, the traditional student is emmeshed in a major period of maturing – another source of instability and change. Even the college senior, with considerably more developed capabilities than the prospective freshman, often lacks much of the necessary perspective on life after college that needs to be brought into many institutional marketing decisions.

Even the recruitment-admissions process cannot be tailored too completely to desires that may be expressed by the traditional student. It is understandable that a student might wish to have this process be easy, riskless, and inexpensive. And yet some consumers' stated desires may not only obscure but even run counter to some of the real developmental needs of young adults. This is not to suggest that some improvements cannot be made.[14]

A delicate balance will have to be struck. A great deal can be learned from students about whether we are communicating effectively with them and addressing their concerns, apprehensions, and interests. However, we also need to address their misperceptions and their limited perceptions. Unnecessary and unproductive individual anxiety and inconvenience in the admissions process should not be perpetrated simply for the operational convenience of educational institutions. Nevertheless, admissions personnel and educational program designers will do a serious disservice to a variety of higher education consumers if the expressed interests of prospective students become a principal foundation for curricular and admissions decisions. We must also look after the interests of a number of "absentee consumers" with real interests in the marketing decisions of higher education: the student who emerges from the educational process greatly changed from the high school senior who selects a type of college, a specific institution, and a course of study; the society and the economy that need the services of a highly educated citizenry; and the society that requires the pursuit of truth regardless of the popular fads or fashions of the times. These are all interests that must be protected and served even though they are not well accommodated in the current concepts and practices of marketing.

The preceding observations are often more relevant to the traditional student than to the mature adult consumer of educational services. It is even true, however, that most prospective adult consumers will have a restricted a priori appreciation of the nature of quality in educational services or of what is possible and desirable as a result of an educational activity.[15] A certain suspension of presumed authority by the consumer is necessary in any decision to seek education and the authority must be vested in the professionals who deliver the services. Marketers often undermine this necessary relationship by projecting too much authority onto the consumer who is making the "purchase decision." Marketers in higher education will have to become comfortable with the need to educate the consumer, to varying degrees, as well as to be responsive to his or her desires. As Barbara Uehling stressed (see pages 137-38), institutions of higher education often will be most responsive to the *needs* of its clientele by displacing or expanding the desires of which they are aware.

A final issue regarding consumers joins marketers' misapprehension of the products of higher education with their failures to take into account the nature of the consumer of education. It has been suggested that gimmicky promotions are not unethical, merely inappropriate (page 54). By being inappropriate, however, I believe they are also unethical to the extent that they fail to represent fully the complexities and subtleties of the educational process and its benefits, and the requirements that educational activities place upon the consumer in order to realize their benefits. Promotion that fails to present or lead people to these issues is misleading, and even marketing experts acknowledge that it is unethical to mislead.

The Firm. Christopher Lovelock and Michael Rothschild have added an important dimension to our consideration of marketing in higher education by underscoring the fact that it is a service industry and by specifying the particular marketing problems that services involve (pages 37-41).

Extending their discussion, I would emphasize the nature of the particular service personnel upon which colleges rely – the faculty. Faculty are professionals. As such, they know more about the current state of the particular technologies (i.e., the disciplines) for the production of their products (e.g., knowledge) than do many of the administrators in their institutions. Faculty are socialized to strong professional norms that protect educational quality. Society has delegated a major responsibility to faculty to represent the interests of many of higher education's absentee consumers, and to do it in accordance with the standards of their disciplines; academic freedom is testimony to these delegated responsibilities. Faculty must make major marketing decisions if the quality of the colleges' products and services is to be maintained.[16] The management of the production and marketing functions in higher education is therefore much more diffuse and complex than marketers generally have recognized.

Another aspect of the educational "firm" that marketers fail to appreciate fully is that students serve a production function as well as being consumers. Studies of college environments have found that a principal source of informal learning for students is their fellow students, and in many educational environments, students are actively used in seminars or discussion groups as educational resources. Thus, the marketing activities of colleges will necessarily be used to attract not only fee-paying customers, as in many other types of firms, but also certain types of students who will contribute to the educational services of the college. Financial aid, and price discounting through merit scholarships, have been designed in part with these institutional needs in mind. The most overt recognition that students contribute to a college, however, is the capacity colleges have to accept prospective consumers for service (and refuse service to others) through the admissions decision. In addition to excluding students who are likely to have difficulty in a given program, admissions permits colleges to select a diverse set of student resources. One of the most serious consequences of marketers' insufficient academic sensibilities is a failure to communicate the responsibilities of students and the expectations that will be placed on them, both as learners and as *fellow learners*, with the same vigor that the benefits of a college are promoted.

Marketers also fail to appreciate fully the complex tension between diversity and specialization that exists within any educational institution. Their frequent counsel to choose the specific market segments that an institution can serve and to establish a clear, distinctive identity or position in the market are important considerations, but far too simplistic to be of great value. Education thrives on broad diversity within an institution that runs counter to much market segmentation and positioning advice.[17] The efforts of colleges to recruit a diverse student body, the distribution requirements that attend most liberal education curricula, and the perennial struggle to implement and sustain interdisciplinary programs are all evidence of the necessity of a degree of nonspecialization in colleges. Another constraint on specialization and distinctiveness comes from the need to have institutions adhere to the basic, common requirements of a liberal education.

Communications, location and timing of programs, pedagogical technique, and to a certain extent, program content will have to be targeted to specific audiences. Distinctive institutional approaches to common problems will be desirable both for institutions – since creativity invigorates – and for the system – because diversity, which results from some specialization, creates certain efficiencies. Efforts to achieve distinctiveness necessarily will be conjoined, however, with the need to pursue the benefits of common academic requirements and high standards. This is simply more evidence that the marketing of colleges and universities involves particularly complex and exciting challenges – a richness of opportunity and obligation not yet fully appreciated by the pioneer importers of formal marketing principles and practices into higher education.

The Market. Marketers have turned their attention to all manner of nonprofit organizations and begun to market their ideas and services to government agencies, educational and health institutions, philanthropic organizations, political figures, and religious organizations. Although the characteristics that differentiate profit and nonprofit organizations have been examined by the nonprofit marketing theorists and some attention given to the marketing implications of these differences,[18] the full significance of the basic defects in nonprofit markets and the way in which nonprofit status protects consumers in such markets has yet to be appreciated.

Some important work in this area has been begun by the Yale University Program on Non-Profit Organizations. Hansmann has examined the rationale for the persistence of nonprofit organizations in an economy where profit-making organizations generally provide maximum social and economic efficiency. He includes higher education as one of several spheres of activity that constitute *defective* markets, which place some major constraints on marketing activities. These constraints are necessary in order to protect the quality of services rendered in markets where consumers cannot easily judge quality or seek redress for failure to deliver expected quality.[19] It will be important to develop academic marketing in the context of this nonprofit-sector theory. That is, both marketers and educators will have to determine what the market deficiencies that cause colleges and universities to be nonprofit organizations mean for the conduct of academic-marketing activities.

Marketers bring their principles and practices to higher education from markets where competition is a major driving force, constrained primarily by external regulation and market forces. Since they generally work for individual firms, marketers' concerns are with the competitive advantage that their craft can bring to specific institutions. However, cooperation, as was discussed above, is an essential aspect of the higher education industry, along with the competition that results in innovations and, at some levels, increased quality. The delicate balance between cooperation and competition within the system must be maintained and the activities of marketers must promote this essential dialectic, not just one aspect.

Pricing is a major component of any marketing mix. The academic market, however, involves some singular pricing practices. Because important benefits of higher education are public goods, price discounting has been developed to encourage equal access among students with varying abilities to pay for an education. Whereas in other spheres of marketing such particularistic pricing would be halted by government action, in higher education the government is a full partner in these programs to promote participation through need-based aid. The kinds of competition-oriented, discriminatory pricing practices (merit scholarships, etc.) that are currently spreading through the system (pages 87-89) pose a threat of serious dislocation in this need-based aid system; to call such practices "aid" is highly dubious. Although legitimately related to institutional desires to obtain a varied set of students, these non-need-based practices operate under protection of a system that has very different functions. The two approaches to discounting should be clearly disentangled, and the value of discounting for reasons other than financial need weighed carefully against its costs to the system (e.g., the increase in competition and the erosion of public willingness to support the need-based system).[20] Costs to the personal development of students must also be considered (e.g., is it good to have relatively immature minds be the object of institutional bidding for their "services"?).[21] At present practice is rapidly outstripping principle and thoughtful deliberation about effects.

Failures of Professional Practice. Many of the problems encountered when marketers attempt to serve the field of higher education or when academic administrators seek the assistance of marketers could be alleviated if marketing practice conformed more closely to marketing rhetoric. Two major discrepancies between practice and principle stand out.

Marketing stresses the desirability of understanding a market before engaging in marketing activities. As discussed above, it is apparent that the ambition of nonprofit marketers has outrun their understanding of the academic market to which they were addressing their message. This problem has often been obscured by the initial receptivity to their message by administrators who are deeply worried about the spectres that loom on the demographic horizon. It is time to step back from a wholesale marketing of Marketing to more serious study of the market and examination of marketing practice as applied to higher education. This is a task that could benefit from the efforts of marketers as well as of academicians.

The second shortcoming of the marketers is their failure to attend to both the *needs* and the *desires* of the consumer. Marketing textbooks recognize the distinction and affirm the necessity of considering both aspects of demand in the design of goods and services and in their delivery. The texts even recognize that the consumer may be unaware of his or her real needs and that short-term desires may well compromise long-term well-being, both for the individual and for society. As noted above, the desires of educational consumers are often naive and perhaps even opposed to needs that will be truly liberating and result in the greatest social benefit.

Although marketers pay rhetorical tribute to the distinctions between needs and desires, and may even go as far as to assign primacy to needs,[22] their technology focuses on consumer desires and their practice tends to make institutions responsive to desires. The marketing craft is full of techniques for finding out what people want and then delivering it to them at a price they will pay. Marketing draws upon survey research, group interviews, and analysis of buying behavior; it does not utilize, to any significant extent, philosophers and social or psychological theoreticians who address questions of the good, noble, or well-lived life.

In addition to not having effective techniques for assessing needs as well as desires, marketing also has failed to develop adequate principles and techniques for effectively incorporating both needs *and* desires into marketing decisions, and for the resolution of conflicts between these two bases for institutional responsiveness. It is possible that the serious and responsible development of marketing in higher education could in turn benefit the entire practice of marketing in our society by attending to these issues.

Where Does Marketing Fit In?

Although business reputedly has moved from a product orientation, through a sales orientation, to a marketing orientation, higher education marketing will have to embrace vigorously all three orientations simultaneously. We will have to uphold the integrity and quality of the product as defined by professional judgment; we will have to promote the ideals, benefits, and requirements of high quality education; and we will have to tailor our messages, prices, and delivery systems to reach and effectively include a wide variety of people in our system of higher education.

We have much to learn from marketing. Market research provides some powerful analytic resources for understanding people and their behavior, and for understanding the relationships among suppliers of goods and services and between suppliers and con-sumers. Business marketing has often achieved more effective ap-plication of psychological principles and learning theory than has education. Of the four components of the marketing mix, the mar-keting principles and practices relating to promotion, pricing, and delivery of services are of greater relevance to higher education than business practices relating to product development.

The promotion of quality education is a serious challenge in a democratic society. The education and motivation of people (read promotion) to want to invest in the liberalizing benefits of educa-tion (instead of in narrow vocational preparation or in more and more consumer goods and services) is no mean task. We need to draw on the experience of profit-oriented firms that have already expended considerable effort to study people and to develop tech-niques for motivating them. The misuse of promotional principles in much of the mass media does not mean that they are without value. As Laurence Veysey suggested, promotion, carefully adapted and supplemented, could do a great deal to raise the level of ap-preciation of education in our society (pages 18-19).

Likewise, our understanding of consumer economic decisions and their perceptions of the economic aspects of higher education can help us price academic offerings. The risk of using discriminatory price incentives in ways that provide more benefit to institutions than to individuals is high, but our greater understanding of such practices should help us avoid the negative aspects.

Our delivery systems and practices can undoubtedly stand im-provements. The technology of higher education has not changed significantly during a period of profound technological, social, and cultural changes in our society. The physical location of educational opportunities and the timing of their availability, as well as the im-provement of pedagogy (especially through the use of modern tech-nology), are all marketing opportunities that could provide tremen-dous individual and social benefits. We also need to develop much more efficient and effective ways of ascertaining students' educa-tional needs and learning behavior and teaching to them. Business marketing has often more consciously and effectively applied learn-ing theory in its affairs than has higher education.

William Ihlanfeldt has suggested that "the future emphasis on marketing in higher education is more likely to be upon product de-velopment than the continued enhancement of the promotional process" (page 90). Such developments should not be according to business marketing principles, however; product decisions in higher education should continue to be primarily professional judgments based on intellectual criteria.[23] Nevertheless, there is great and increasing need to relate these decisions to the market. Certainly the liberal arts need to incorporate much more of our technological culture *and its technology* than they generally do. Although professional faculty members are the most knowledgeable about the central intellectual components of a college's products and services, and therefore the essential locus of many of the marketing decisions, there are serious flaws in the way faculty marketing activities are conducted. Faculty know a great deal about what needs to be marketed; however, they are neither prepared for nor expected to understand much about markets or the processes of marketing. Little information is brought into their decision-making processes, beyond their own immediate experiences, about the perceptions, prejudices, and desires of people in the market. A major marketing problem for higher education administrators is to devise ways of making the faculty aware of the market, and rewarding them for effective attention to market realities.

One resource for helping institutions and faculty become more responsive to market needs and desires would be the more effective involvement of alumni in curricular advisory councils and more frequent alumni surveys. Unless we have failed miserably at our jobs, alumni should bring to the process an appreciation of higher education and its character, a respect for particular institutions, and a perspective on the market beyond the campus. Faculty should have the benefit of these perspectives to relate to the intellectual phenomena of which they are custodians.

Closing Observations

The problems and challenges facing higher education are profound. Our colleges and universities will have to continue their long tradition of marketing their services — and they will have to do it well. Undoubtedly the powerful concepts and practices of professional marketers — particularly market analysis — can contribute greatly to these efforts. The development of marketing practices in higher education will have to occur, however, in a manner that is consistent with the particular nature and responsibilities of higher education and its publics. These developments must take place cautiously and sensitively, else we risk damage to the health of the intellectual capacity in our society or at least wasted resources. I see great value in the existing intellectual functions of higher education, and this paper is in part a warning against sources of potential erosion of their integrity; at the same time I would argue that some aspects of marketing can help colleges discharge these functions more effectively without suffering the adverse consequences of other aspects. Both marketers and the higher education community need to give serious and extensive examination to the issues noted and develop appropriate sensibilities to both the market and the nature of higher education. Each new marketing practice must be subjected to scrutiny for its effects on institutions, individuals (particularly students), and the system. Although we share attributes and problems with other organizations in society, our marketing will require an indigenous cast. As it has in the past, academic marketing will often have to respond to needs not yet felt by society or individuals.

The colloquium that precipitated this paper, and therefore the paper, was focused on marketing as it affects college admissions. This question is really part of a larger issue for the eighties, however – how do we market the surplus intellectual and physical resources that our college campuses are about to represent? These resources are surplus only in the sense that the potential for their traditional use is being temporarily constrained. Certainly one answer in a labor-intensive industry, where quality is partly a function of the amount of labor invested in the process, could be to increase the quality of the services (e.g., lower student-faculty ratios). That would necessarily increase costs – and the promotion of higher quality with higher costs would be a formidable challenge (although maybe no less than our professional ideals should accept).

There are other approaches, however. Our campuses are not just places where students are taught; they are reservoirs of some of our nation's finest intellectual resources. Our present challenge is to find ways of using these resources – perhaps in business, in government, in community service – that both obtain immediate benefits and do not compromise the long-term national stock of independent intellectual capacity and activity. For example, might the services of academic psychologists, philosophers, or English teachers be used on a part-time basis in business to carry on scholarship, research, or teaching? Undoubtedly, as with any remarketing undertaking of this magnitude, some retooling and retraining will be necessary. What is important is to market these resources in ways that also protect the processes by which we search for truth, however unpopular or esoteric. Pervasive sensibilities to the nature of intellectual activity will have to be cultivated, for it appears that the time is not far off when a good portion of these currently surplus resources will be needed again in their traditional roles.

Trustees who govern an institution of higher education and the staff who operate it hold a trust that transcends their particular college. Institutional marketing decisions must be made with this transcendent trust in mind. In a period when there is a temporary decline in a major traditional means of support (students) for the institutions that provide our society's intellectual resources, we must find ways to preserve, nuture, and advance — to market — these essential civilized capacities. These are questions that transcend whether an individual college survives; these are challenges of more enduring consequence.

In *The Marketing Mystique*, McKay asks businesses to decide whether they are organized to maintain tradition, to satisfy the internal convenience of the business, or to serve customers effectively.[24] He sees these orientations as incompatible and suggests the need for a choice. Higher education's answer must differ from the one he commends to business. If we change "convenience" to "requirements," the answer for colleges must be, "We will pursue all three, for they are interdependent."

References

1. Frederick Rudolph, *The American College and University: A History.* New York: Vintage Books, 1965, Chapters 3, 10, 15.

2. Some marketing theorists have suggested that the marketing concept now being promoted to higher education has already outlived much of its usefulness to business. See Martin L. Bell and C. William Emory, "The Faltering Marketing Concept," pp. 62-72 in *Controversy and Dialog in Marketing*, Ross Lawrence Gobel and Roy T. Shaw, editors. Englewood Cliffs, N.J.: Prentice-Hall, Inc., 1975. Also Frederick E. Webster, Jr., *Social Aspects of Marketing.* Englewood Cliffs, N.J.: Prentice-Hall, Inc., 1974, p. 110.

3. College Entrance Examination Board. *A Role for Marketing in College Admissions.* New York: College Entrance Examination Board, 1976.

4. Council for the Advancement of Small Colleges, *A Marketing Approach to Program Development.* Washington, D.C.: Council for the Advancement of Small Colleges, 1978. William Ihlanfeldt, "A Management Approach to the Buyer's Market," *Liberal Education*, May 1975, pp. 133-148. Philip Kotler, "Strategies for Introducing Marketing into Nonprofit Organizations," *Journal of Marketing*, Vol. 43, January 1979, pp. 37-44.

5. Larry Litten, "Marketing Higher Education: Benefits and Risks for the American Academic System," *Journal of Higher Education*, Vol. LI, January/February 1980, pp. 40-59.

6. Philip Kotler and Sidney J. Levy, "Broadening the Concept of Marketing," *Journal of Marketing*, Vol. 43, January 1969, p. 15.

7. Edward B. Fiske, "The Marketing of the Colleges," *Atlantic Monthly*, October 1979, pp. 93-98.

8. Theodore Marchese, Talk to American Association for Higher Education, quoted in *Higher Education Daily*, April 20, 1979.

9. See the definitions given on pages 44-45 and 133. Shelby D. Hunt notes and defends this definitional morass ("The Nature and Scope of Marketing," *Journal of Marketing*, Vol. 40, July 1976, pp. 17-28). Webster, on the other hand, criticizes some of the loose usage (*Social Aspects of Marketing*, pp. 89-92).

10. Philip Kotler, *Marketing for Non-Profit Organizations*. Englewood Cliffs, N.J.: Prentice-Hall, Inc., 1975, p. 52.

11. Other marketing theorists with a basic appreciation of some of the special features of academic markets include Paul Hugstad, "The Marketing Concept in Higher Education: A Caveat," *Liberal Education*, Vol. 61, December 1975, pp. 504-512, and Eugene Fram, "Marketing Higher Education," pp. 56-67 in *The Future in the Making*, D.W. Vermilye, editor. San Francisco: Jossey-Bass, Inc., Publishers, 1973.

12. Cf. Norman W. Storer, *The Social System of Science*. New York: Holt, Rinehart and Winston, 1966, Chapters 4 and 5. It should be noted that consensus does not imply unanimity nor preclude differing schools of thought.

13. Gordon H. Lewis and Sue Morrison conducted a study for the U.S. Navy on decision processes for "unique decisions"—decisions that are "being made by the decision maker for the first time, the outcome of [which] is usually relatively important to the decision maker, and typically the decision maker not only lacks information about alternatives and about how they rank on particular attributes, but he or she is not even sure what the 'important' attributes of a good decision would be." They chose the college selection process as the focus for this study. "A Longitudinal Study of College Selection." Technical Report #2. School of Urban and Public Affairs, Carnegie-Mellon University, Pittsburg, Penna., February 1975, processed, p. 1.

14. Herbert Sacks, "Bloody Monday: The Crises of the High School Senior," pp. 10-47 in *Hurdles: The Admissions Dilemma in American Higher Education*, Herbert Sacks and Associates, editors. New York: Atheneum, 1978.

15. See Howard R. Bowen, *Adult Learning, Higher Education, and the Economics of Unused Capacity*. New York: College Entrance Examination Board, 1980.

16. In the Supreme Court decision in the *National Labor Relations Board* v. *Yeshiva University*, both sides recognized the integral role of faculty in college marketing decisions—the majority put faculty firmly on the management team; the minority opinion suggested that faculty make marketing decisions in their own professional interests. *Chronicle of Higher Education*, February 25, 1980, pp. 1, 7-9.

17. Roy E. Licklider has also noted these endemic tensions in higher education ("Faculty Ethics in Academic Depression," pp. 118-142 in *Disorders in Higher Education*, Clarence Walton and Frederick deW. Bolman, editors. Englewood Cliffs, N.J.: Prentice-Hall, Inc., 1979). He and Paul Hugstad have both also warned against pseudo-differentiation in colleges and their programs in the interests of creating a

special identity ("The Marketing Concept in Higher Education: A Caveat," *Liberal Education*, December 1975, pp. 504-512).

18. Christopher Lovelock and Charles B. Weinberg, "Contrasting Public and Private Sector Marketing," pp. 27-32 in *Readings in Public and Non-Profit Marketing*, Christopher Lovelock and Charles Weinberg, editors. [Palo Alto, Calif.]: The Scientific Press, 1978.

19. Henry Hansmann, "The Role of Non-Profit Enterprise." *Yale Law Journal*, Vol. 89, April 1980, pp. 835-901.

20. Humphry Doerman was the first to call the author's attention to these concerns in a private conversation.

21. Since we've been bidding on bodies for our athletic machines for years, it might be argued that academic merit scholarships introduce a desirable corrective balance to the system. Perhaps so. It also seems to hold the potential of infecting a new part of the system with many of the evils of another part.

22. Cf. Kotler's "societal marketing concept," (*Marketing for Non-Profit Organizations*, p. 18) or Eugene J. Kelley's "meta-marketing" ("Ethics and Science in Marketing," pp. 82-83 in *Managerial Marketing Perspectives and Viewpoints*, 3rd edition, Eugene T. Kelley and William Lazar, editors. Homewood, Ill.: Richard D. Irwin, Inc., 1967.)

23. Again, postsecondary vocational training or cultural enrichment activities, as opposed to higher education, can and should have a more market-oriented product-development process, supported by professional standards of quality.

24. Edward McKay. N.p.: American Management Association, 1972, p. 33.

List of Participants

Alverno College:
Lois Rice
  Director of College Relations

American Association of Collegiate
Registrars and Admissions Officers:
Albert L. Clary
  Director, Academic Services
  Louisiana State University
J. Douglas Conner
  Executive Director
Howard B. Shontz
  Vice President for Admissions/
  Financial Aid
  University of California, Berkeley

American Association of Community
and Junior Colleges:
John J. Deady
  Vice President — Student Services
  Milwaukee Area Technical College

American Association of State
Colleges and Universities:
Charles J. Graham
  President
  St. Cloud State University

American Council on Education:
Cathy Henderson
  Research Associate

American Marketing Association:
Patrick E. Murphy
  Assistant Professor of Marketing
  Marquette University

Association of Catholic Colleges
and Universities:
Sister Alice Gallin
  Associate Executive Director

Beloit College:
Zeddie Bowen
  Provost
Howard Hildebrandt
  Student
  Wingspread Fellow

Boston College:
John J. Maguire
  Dean of Admissions, Records, and
  Financial Aid

Carleton College:
Mark Crawford
  Student
  Wingspread Fellow

The Chronicle of Higher Education:
Lorenzo Middleton
  Assistant Editor

The College Board:
Arthur Doyle
  Director
  Midwestern Regional Office
George H. Hanford
  President
Darrell R. Morris
  Executive Associate
Diane L. Olsen
  Managing Editor, Publications

Consortium on Financing Higher
Education:
Larry H. Litten
  Associate Director

Cooperative Education Association:
E. R. Pettebone
  Executive Secretary

The Council for the Advancement of
Small Colleges:
Father Thomas Finucan
  President
  Viterbo College

The Council on Post-secondary
Accreditation:
Dorothy G. Peterson
  Staff Associate/Consultant

Education Commission of the States:
Lou Rabineau
  Director of Advanced Leadership
  Program Service

The Ford Foundation:
Fred E. Crossland
  Program Officer

Harvard University:
Stephen K. Bailey
  Professor of Education and Social
  Policy
  Graduate School of Education

Indiana University/Purdue University
at Indianapolis:
Georgia Ann Schockley
  Student
  Wingspread Fellow

Kalamazoo College:
Dale Methven
  Student
  Wingspread Fellow

The Lindenwood Colleges:
Frank W. Hetherington
  Director of Admissions and Student
  Aid

Michigan State University:
Maurice A. Crane
  Professor of Humanities

Moton Consortium on Admissions and
Financial Aid:
Mary T. Coleman
  Director

National Association of College
Admissions Counselors:
James A. Alexander, Jr.
  Counselor
  Highland Park High School
Ann P. Fritts
  Director of Guidance Counseling
  The Lovett School
Robert G. McLendon
  Dean of Admissions
  Brevard College
Charles A. Marshall
  Executive Director
Helen J. Pape
  Director of Professional Education

National Association of College and
University Business Officers
Student-Related Activities Committee:
Kenneth Brown
  Millikin University

National Association of Foreign Student
Affairs:
Mary Cay Martin
  Director of International Student
  Services
  The University of Chicago

National Association of Independent
Colleges and Universities:
George N. Rainsford
  President
  Kalamazoo College

National Association of Secondary
School Principals:
Warren M. McGregor
  Secondary School Principal
  Manhasset Junior–Senior High
  School

New England Board of Higher
Education:
John C. Hoy
  Executive Director

The New York Times:
Gene J. Maeroff
  National Education Correspondent

Northwestern University:
William Ihlanfeldt
  Vice President
  Institutional Relations
Gretchen Van Riper
  Student
  Wingspread Fellow

Pennsylvania Department of Education:
Marna C. Whittington
  Deputy Secretary, Research, Planning
  and Data Management

Project CHOICE:
David Chapman
  Associate Director

State University of New York, Albany:
Douglas M. Windham
  Professor of Education

University of California, Santa Cruz:
Laurence Veysey
  Professor of History

The University of Chicago:
Charles D. O'Connell, Jr.
  Vice President and Dean of Student
  Affairs

University of Missouri, Columbia:
Barbara S. Uehling
  Chancellor and Professor
  Department of Psychology

University of New Hampshire:
Eugene A. Savage
  Dean of Admissions

University of Pennsylvania:
Robert Zemsky
  Director of Higher Education Finance
  Research Institute

University of Wisconsin, Eau Claire:
Robert D. Sather
  Director, Financial Aid

University of Wisconsin, Madison:
Michael L. Rothschild
  Associate Professor of Business

University of Wisconsin System:
Roland Baldwin
  Director of Student Services
  University of Wisconsin Center–
  Washington County
Kris Heffernan
  Counselor
  Higher Education Location Program

APf